# Finding English Law:

## Quick Access to Key Titles

### Second Edition



William S. Hein & Co., Inc.
Getzville, New York
2017

*Publisher's Cataloging in Publication Data*

Names: Eaton, John, 1953- author.

Title: Finding English law : quick access to key titles / by John Eaton.

Description: Second edition. | Getzville, New York : William S. Hein & Co., Inc., 2017. | Revision of the author's "Finding English law" (London : Wildy, Simmonds & Hill, 2011).

Identifiers: ISBN: 978-0-8377-4052-2 | LCCN: 2017931911

Subjects: LCSH: Law--Great Britain--Bibliography. | Law--England--Bibliography. | Law--Wales--Bibliography. | Law--European Union countries--Bibliography. | LCGFT: Bibliographies. | Informational works.

Classification: LCC: KD51 .E28 2017 | DDC: 016.34/00942--dc23



Printed in the United States of America

This volume is printed on acid-free paper
by William S. Hein & Co., Inc.

## TABLE OF CONTENTS

# INTRODUCTION TO THE SECOND EDITION

In the first edition of this book, I revealed that I am a fervent believer that efficient legal research begins with consulting leading secondary sources, which most often are comprehensive, current textbooks. Those of us who live in the "Legal Anglosphere" (that is, jurisdictions where the bases and foundations of our law originated in England) frequently have cause to consult English textbooks but as we are not overly familiar with these titles, we struggle to identify which works merit our trust. Moreover, we are occasionally bemused by differences in terminology and law between England and our own jurisdiction. This book is intended to assist with these particular challenges by providing a quick, thumbnail description of the law (statutory and jurisprudential) in ninety-seven different legal topics and a list of leading texts relevant to each. This is a list of relevant works and is not an evaluative undertaking. Although I am not familiar with all titles listed herein, I have made sure to include every title that I know from experience or reputation to be a leading work on its topic. This book's intention is to be neither a textbook itself nor a bibliography of English law; its aims are more modest and it seeks only to provide necessary first-instance assistance to researchers into English law who have little or no familiarity with the discipline and its materials.

It is important to be aware of the distinction between United Kingdom law and English law. This work deals specifically with the latter because for the most part it was English law that was transported to the corners of the world by way of the British Empire. The law of jurisdictions such as the United States, Canada, Australia, and New Zealand, among others, grew specifically out of English law with little influence from Scotland or Northern Ireland. As a result, titles which are singularly Scottish or Northern Irish have been excluded; however a great number of the titles listed hereunder are British in scope and will therefore incorporate their law. Titles which are exclusively related to Welsh law have also been excluded but for the great majority of matters the law of England *is* the law of Wales and so most of these titles do in effect include Welsh law. Another jurisdiction to note—for the short-term, at least—is that of the European Union. There are, of course, many textbooks dealing with European Union law and regulations. Unless a title is specifically geared to the law of England it is excluded. For the most part, references to the European Union can be found in the thumb-nail descriptions of the law in instances where there are relevant European regulations, directives, and decisions. Given that Britain's exit from the union won't likely be effected until sometime between 2018 and 2020, the regulations and directives of the European Union remain in vigour at time of this writing.

In this edition I have expanded the scope of the book somewhat by including where possible a list of noteworthy websites, blogs, and databases. It has proved a challenge to include the appropriate digital resources as they are usually less formal and doctrinal than the textbooks listed in the book; however, care has been taken to include ones that are instructive and sufficiently specific to a particular topic to warrant inclusion. While it is demonstrably helpful to the reader to include such resources it is important to note that most of the websites and blogs included are aimed more at practitioners than researchers and often deal more with strategic practice issues than they do with substantive law. However, many of them serve as very valuable current awareness services and can be used as "early warning systems" for changes and developments in English law. It is apparent—but not surprising—that the topics generating the most social media "heat" are those that deal with issues relevant to digital information, such as Information Technology Law, Data Protection, Freedom of Information, and Privacy Law, *inter alia.* Employment & Labour Law and Family Law are other areas of considerable online activity. However, there is a dearth of appropriate online sources on some of the more established doctrinal areas of law such Contracts and general treatments of Tort law. Readers wishing to find useful compilations of blogs and websites devoted to English law should consult Nick Holmes's *Lawfinder* website (http://www.infolaw.co.uk/lawfinder/) and Delia Venables's *100 Best Legal Blogs, UK & Ireland* (http://www.venables.co.uk/blogs.htm).

The listings of the titles in this work are essentially in reverse chronological order (newest first). Those that are published in loose leaf form are listed first, under the assumption that they will be the most current. Thereafter the list is by year and within each year, alphabetical by author's surname. Accompanying each entry is a notation which will inform the reader as to the most appropriate audience for each title. Those followed by [A] are for academics, [P] for practitioners, [S] for students, and [N] for non-practitioners. Many titles are applicable to more than one such group in which case all appropriate designators will be listed. Where titles also exist as an eBook, an icon of a computer mouse gives indication that this is so.

No legal subject is watertight and therefore within most of the ninety-seven topics listed in this work there is reference to 'Related topics' which will assist the reader in expanding their survey of titles. This work was written between 2015 and 2016 and therefore the titles listed are current as to that period of time.

With regard to spelling, I have employed the spelling that is most commonly found in the countries comprising the "legal Anglosphere" namely, British spelling. Therefore the reader will encounter –our (e.g., 'labour') as opposed to –or; –re (as in 'centre' and 'theatre') as opposed to –er; and –nce ('defence', 'licence') as opposed to –nse.

As was the case with the first edition, I am confident that there is considerable utility in this work. It will orient the researcher to the key titles of all manner of English law while providing a digestible account of the underlying law of each and its governing legislation or legal grounding. It may also prove to be a valuable collection development tool to librarians and others charged with developing collections of leading English legal materials.

# ACKNOWLEDGEMENTS

The second edition of this book would not have come into being were it not for the publication staff at W.S. Hein & Company, particularly senior editor Sheila Jarrett. Without her encouragement and flexibility this edition may not have come to fruition. Thanks are also owed to Shannon Hein for his encouragement and support in pursuit of this project.

While conducting research in the United Kingdom for this book I was assisted by the generosity and hospitality of Steven and Elaine Ross, who provided me shelter, and by Guy Holborn, Catherine McArdle, and the staff of the wonderful law library at Lincoln's Inn in London for welcoming me and allowing me space and access to their marvellous collection. I tip my hat to all of them and say a hearty "thanks for everything." Finally, I continue to receive helpful and welcome counsel from legal publisher Brian Hill of Wildy, Simmonds & Hill in London and I thank him therefor.

Finally, I would not have been able to pursue this project were it not for the fact that my "regular job" and "everyday life" were left to such reliable trustees. I am grateful to Donna Sikorsky for so capably managing the E.K. Williams Law Library in my absence. I also profusely thank my wonderful wife, Ellen, for continuing to maintain a perfect home during my frequent and lengthy absences.

John Eaton
Winnipeg, Canada
March, 2016

# GLOSSARY & GUIDE

Titles are arranged in reverse chronological order of publication date (newest first).

## Publication Information

**LL** = Looseleaf publication. These works are comprised of looseleaf pages in a binder style cover which are frequently updated by the removal of out-of-date pages and the insertion of updated pages.

* = Periodic supplements. A year followed by an asterisk (e.g., 2011*) indicates that the original edition was published in 2011 but has been supplemented by updates since.

**Annual** = Titles which are published on an annual basis.

= An eBook is available for this title.

## Appropriate Readership

**[A]** = Academic publication. Most appropriate for use by legal academics, scholars, and for in-depth research.

**[P]** = Practice-oriented publication. Most appropriate for practitioners of law in researching the substantive and procedural law of a particular topic.

**[S]** = Student publication. Most appropriate for students learning the rudiments of a specific legal subject.

**[N]** = Appropriate for the non-lawyer.

Some titles are appropriate for more than one readership and will be noted as such.

## ABOUT THE AUTHOR

John Eaton enjoyed a 25-year career as Law Librarian and Professor at the Universities of Manitoba and Western Ontario. He was President of the Canadian Association of Law Libraries from 2001 to 2003 and was the recipient of that association's Denis Marshall Memorial Award for Excellence in Law Librarianship in 2006. In 2012 he was awarded the Association of College Research Libraries Marta Lange/Sage-CQ Press Award for distinguished contributions to bibliography and information service in Law. Currently he is the North American representative of the English legal bookseller and publisher Wildy & Sons Ltd. He resides in Winnipeg, Manitoba.

# ACCOUNTING LAW

This topic refers to the law as it relates to accountants, auditors, and other preparers of financial statements and deals mostly with the legal requirements of their activities and liabilities for failure to meet accepted standards. There is, in fact, very little "law" in this topic given that the standards which must be met are not generally found in legislation (other than a few sections of the Companies Act 2006), but rather in a variety of standards and practices created by the Accounting Standards Committee and Accounting Standards Board and adopted by the accountancy profession such as UK GAAP (generally accepted accounting principles in the UK), Statements of Standard Accounting Practice (SSAPs), and Financial Reporting Standards (FSRs). There is a substantial body of jurisprudence assisting in the interpretation and application of these practices.

Standards for auditors are found in GAAS (Generally Accepted Auditing Standards) and ISAs (International Standard on Auditing).

*Related topic(s): COMMERCIAL LAW; COMPANY LAW; PROFESSIONAL CONDUCT and ETHICS; PROFESSIONAL NEGLIGENCE.*

| Author(s) | Title | Edition | Publisher | Year |
|---|---|---|---|---|
| | *Auditing and Reporting 2015-16* [P] | | CCH Editions | Annual |
| Lloyd, Helen, *et al.* | *Applying New UK GAAP 2015-16: A Practical Guide to Financial Reporting* [P] | | CCH Editions | Annual |
| Lole, James, ed. | *Accounting Standards 2015-16* [P] | | CCH Editions | Annual |
| Pricewaterhouse Coopers LLP | *Manual of Accounting: UK GAAP* [P] | 2nd | Bloomsbury Professional | Annual |
| Salzedo, Simon and Singla, Tony | *Accountants' Negligence and Liability* [P,N] | | Bloomsbury Professional | 2016 |
| Watson-Gandy, Mark | *Watson-Gandy on the Law Relating to Accountants: Law, Precedents, Practice and Procedure* [P] | 2nd | Hammicks | 2008 |
| Holgate, Peter | *Accounting Principles for Lawyers* [P] | | Cambridge University Press | 2006 |

## Noteworthy websites, blogs, etc.:

### WEBSITE

- Fraud Advisory Panel, Resources (https://www.fraudadvisorypanel.org/resource/)
- Institute of Chartered Accounts in England and Wales, ICAEW (www.icaew.com)

# ADMINISTRATIVE LAW

The normal context for this topic includes numerous areas of public or government law and is usually paired with Constitutional Law. This list employs a narrower definition of administrative law and limits it to matters related to the numerous quasi-judicial commissions, boards, tribunals, and public inquiries commonly created or undertaken by government. Important subtopics are *inter alia*: judicial review, including procedural fairness and *ultra vires*; and judicial remedies, such as *habeas corpus* and *quo warranto*.

Important statutory provisions include the Tribunals and Inquiries Act 1992, Supreme Court Act 1981, Senior Courts Act 1981, Crown Proceedings Act 1947, and Civil Jurisdiction and Judgements Act 1982. There are also numerous relevant practice directions supplementing the Civil Procedure Rules.

For titles dealing more specifically with the structure and functioning of government, see CONSTITUTIONAL LAW. For works dealing with Crown Privilege, see CROWN LAW.

*Related topic(s): CONSTITUTIONAL LAW; LOCAL GOVERNMENT LAW.*

| Author(s) | Title | Edition | Publisher | Year |
|---|---|---|---|---|
| Craig, Paul | *Administrative Law* [S,A,P] 🖰 | 8th | Sweet & Maxwell | 2016 |
| Tomkins, Adam | *Public Law* [S] | 2nd | Oxford University Press | 2016 |
| Barnett, Hilaire | *Constitutional & Administrative Law* [S] | 11th | Routledge | 2015 |
| Carroll, Alex | *Constitutional and Administrative Law* [S] | 8th | Pearson Education | 2015 |
| Endicott, Timothy | *Administrative Law* [A] | 3rd | Oxford University Press | 2015 |
| Bradley, A.W., and Ewing, K.D. , and Knight, Christopher | *Constitutional and Administrative Law* [S] | 16th | Pearson Education | 2014 |
| Lewis, Clive, Q.C. | *Judicial Remedies in Public Law* [P] | 5th | Sweet & Maxwell | 2014 |
| Supperstone, Michael, Goudie, James, and Walker, Paul | *Supperstone, Goudie, and Walker: Judicial Review* [P] | 5th | LexisNexis Butterworths | 2014 |

| Author(s) | Title | Edition | Publisher | Year |
|---|---|---|---|---|
| Wade, H.W.R. and Forsyth, C.F. | *Administrative Law* [S,A,P] | 11th | Oxford University Press | 2014 |
| Le Sueur, Andrew, Sunkin, Maurice, and Murkens, Jo | *Public Law: Text, Cases, and Materials* [S] | 2nd | Oxford University Press | 2013 |
| Woolf, The Rt. Hon. Lord, Jowell, Jeffrey, and Le Sueur, Andrew | *De Smith's Judicial Review* [P] | 7th | Sweet & Maxwell | 2013* |
| Fordham, Michael | *Judicial Review Handbook* [P] | 6th | Hart | 2012 |
| Leyland, Peter and Anthony, Gordon | *Textbook on Administrative Law* [S] | 7th | Oxford University Press | 2012 |
| Cane, Peter | *An Introduction to Administrative Law* [S,N] | 5th | Oxford University Press | 2011 |
| Elliott, Mark | *Beatson, Matthews & Elliott's Administrative Law: Text and Materials* [S] | 4th | Oxford University Press | 2011 |
| Feldman, David, ed. | *English Public Law* [A,P] | 2nd | Oxford University Press | 2009 |

## Noteworthy websites, blogs, etc.:

### WEBSITES

- Jordan Publishing, Public Law and Regulation: Case Reports (http://www.jordanpublishing.co.uk/practice-areas/public-law/news_and_comment?filter[category_id]=2433)

### BLOGS

- Fieldfisher (firm), The Public Eye (http://publicregulatoryblog.fieldfisher.com/)
- UK Administrative Justice Institute, Blog (https://ukaji.org/)

# ADVOCACY

Advocacy has long been an essential skill of English lawyers, particularly barristers. At one time the term would have contemplated only oral advocacy as there was long a tradition that decisions were based primarily in response to oral argument rather than written submission. However, this has changed considerably in the last decade or so and now written argument (or at least a written outline of the accompanying oral argument) is becoming more the norm in many matters of litigation. The result of this is that many modern English lawyers need to master two types of legal advocacy, oral and written. There are a number of titles which endeavour to impart these core skills to practitioners.

*Related topic(s): LEGAL SKILLS and METHOD.*

| Author(s) | Title | Edition | Publisher | Year |
|---|---|---|---|---|
| Pope, David and Hill, Dan | *Mooting and Advocacy Skills* [S] | 3rd | Sweet & Maxwell | 2015 |
| McPeake, Robert, ed. | *Bar Manual: Advocacy* [S] | 17th | Oxford University Press | 2014 |
| Bedingfield, David | *Advocacy in Family Proceedings: Theory and Practice* [P] | 2nd | Family Law | 2013 |
| Goodman, Andrew | *Mediation Advocacy* [S,P] | 2nd | Nova Law and Finance | 2011 |
| Evans, Keith | *The Language of Advocacy: What to Say and How to Say It in the English Speaking Courts* [S] | | Oxford University Press | 1998 |
| Du Cann, Richard | *The Art of the Advocate* [S] | 2nd | Penguin | 1995 |
| Evans, Keith | *The Golden Rules of Advocacy* [S] | | Oxford University Press | 1993 |
| Napley, Sir David | *The Technique of Persuasion* [S] | 4th | Sweet & Maxwell | 1992 |
| Munkman, John | *The Technique of Advocacy* [S] | | LexisNexis Butterworths | 1991 |

# AGENCY

In law the term 'agency' is normally used to indicate an arrangement wherein one party, the principal, has empowered another, the agent, to create and maintain legal relationships with other parties on the principal's behalf. A special agent is authorized for a specific purpose whereas a general agent is not so limited. Important subdivisions of agency include the creation of the agency relationship, the agent's powers, the relationships between the principal and agent and the agent and third parties, and the termination of the agency. The law with regard to commercial agencies is predominantly grounded in case law.

Another sphere in which agency arrangements are common is that of mental health and capacity. While most research into this topic is in relation to commercial agencies, arrangements such as power of attorney are also examples of agency relationships. Agency in this context is subject to a number of statutory and regulatory prescriptions such as the Lasting Power of Attorney, Enduring Power of Attorney, and Public Guardian Regulations 2007 pursuant to the Mental Capacity Act 2005.

*Related topic(s): COMMERCIAL LAW; CONTRACT LAW; MEDICAL LAW; MENTAL HEALTH LAW.*

| Author(s) | Title | Edition | Publisher | Year |
|---|---|---|---|---|
| Billins, Roger | *Agency Law* [P] | | Sweet & Maxwell | LL |
| Busch, Danny, Macgregor, Laura, and Watts, Peter, eds. | *Agency Law in Commercial Practice* [P,A] | | Oxford University Press | 2016 |
| Singleton, Susan | *Commercial Agency Agreements: Law and Practice* [P] | 4th | Bloomsbury Professional | 2015 |
| Watts, Peter G., ed. | *Bowstead and Reynolds on Agency* [P,A] | 20th | Sweet & Maxwell | 2014* |
| Bennett, Howard | *Principles of the Law of Agency* [P,S] | | Hart Publishing | 2013 |
| Munday, Roderick | *Agency: Law and Principles* [S] | 2nd | Oxford University Press | 2013 |
| Randolph, Fergus, Q.C. and Davey, Jonathan | *The European Law of Commercial Agency* [A,P] | 3rd | Hart Publishing | 2010 |
| Markesinis, Basil S. and Munday, Roderick | *An Outline of the Law of Agency* [S] | 4th | Oxford University Press | 1998 |

# AGRICULTURE LAW

Works listed under agriculture law—or farm law—deal with the law as it relates to farming but principally in two contexts: agricultural land holdings and marketing of agricultural products. It is an ancient area of law that spent centuries developing within the common law. There is, however, now a large body of statutory law in play.

Along with the issues of land holdings and product marketing other areas of interest included such topics as fertilisers and pesticides, the protection of crops, agricultural pollution, and agricultural labour.

Statutes of note: the Agriculture Act (of which there are numerous enactments with portions still in force: 1947, 1967, 1970, 1986, and 1993), the Agricultural Tenancies Act 1995, the Agricultural Holdings Act 1986, the Farm Land and Rural Development Act 1988, the Small Holdings and Allotments Act 1908, and the Agricultural Marketing Acts of 1958 and 1983. Matters related to agricultural employment in Wales are dealt with in the Agricultural Sector (Wales) Act 2014.

*Related topic(s): ANIMAL LAW; ENVIRONMENTAL LAW; LANDLORD and TENANT LAW; NUISANCE; REAL PROPERTY.*

| Author(s) | Title | Edition | Publisher | Year |
|---|---|---|---|---|
| Davis, Nigel, Smith, Graham, and Sydenham, Angela | *Agricultural Precedents Handbook* [P] | 3rd | Jordan Publishing | 2016 |
| Muir Watt, James and Moss, Joanne R. | *Muir Watt and Ross Agricultural Holdings* [P] | 15th | Sweet & Maxwell | 2016 |
| Rodgers, Christopher P. | *Agricultural Law* [P] | 4th | Bloomsbury Professional | 2016 |
| Feitshans, Theodore A. | *Agricultural and Agribusiness Law: An Introduction for Non-Lawyers* [N] | | Routledge | 2015 |
| Williams, Peter R. | *Scammell, Densham & Williams Law of Agricultural Holdings* [P] | 10th | LexisNexis Butterworths | 2015* |
| Barr, William, Falkner, James, and Slatter, Michelle | *Farm Tenancies* [P,S] | 3rd | Morrow & Co | 2014 |
| Sydenham, Angela | *Agricultural Tenancies* [P] | 2nd | Wildy, Simmonds & Hill | 2009 |

| | | | | |
|---|---|---|---|---|
| Sydenham, Angela and Monnington, Bruce | *Essential Law for Land-owners and Farmers* [N] | 4th | Wiley-Blackwell | 2003 |

# AIR and SPACE LAW

This topic deals with the carriage of passengers and materials by air (and in the latter case, occasionally by spacecraft) and is also known as civil aviation. As such it is largely international in scope but there are domestic British legislative and licensing provisions.

This area of law is primarily informed by statute and international convention. Significant domestic statutes include: the Transport Act 2000, Airports Act 1986, Civil Aviation Act 1980, Civil Aviation Act 1982, Civil Aviation (Eurocontrol) Act 1983, Civil Aviation (Amendment) Act 1996, Aviation Security Act 1982, Aviation and Maritime Security Act 1990, and Aviation Offences Act 2003. There is also a large number of statutory instruments dealing with aviation including, the Air Navigation Order 2005, Air Navigation (General) Regulations 2006, Rules of the Air Regulations 2007, and the Civil Aviation Authority Regulations 1991.

Noteworthy European legislation and international conventions are EC Council Regulation 1008/2008 (common rules for the operation of air services), EC Council Regulation 3922/91, as amended by 859/2008 (harmonisation of technical requirements and administrative procedures in the field of civil aviation),the Convention on International Civil Aviation (Chicago, 1944), and the Convention for the Unification of Certain Rules Relating to International Carriage by Air (Montreal, 1999).

Major subtopics are aircraft (standards, licensing, and operation), airports and aerodromes, and accident investigation.

*Related topic(s): SHIPPING, TRANSPORT, and MARITIME LAW.*

| Author(s) | Title | Edition | Publisher | Year |
|---|---|---|---|---|
| MacLean, J.D., *et. al.* eds. | *Shawcross and Beaumont: Air Law* [P] | | LexisNexis Butterworths | LL |
| McBain, Graham S. | *Aircraft Liens and Detention Rights* [P] | | Sweet & Maxwell | LL |
| Jakhu, Ram and Dempsey, Paul Stephen, eds. | *Routledge Handbook of Space Law* [A,P] | | Routledge | 2016 |
| Pearson, Michael W. and Riley, Daniel S. | *Foundations of Aviation Law* [A] | | Ashgate | 2015 |

| Author(s) | Title | Edition | Publisher | Year |
|---|---|---|---|---|
| Posner, Katherine B., Marland, Tim, and Chrystal, Philip | *Margo on Aviation Insurance* [P] | 4th | Lexis Nexis Butterworths | 2014 |
| Diederiks-Veschoor, I.H. Ph. and Mendes de Leon, Pablo | *An Introduction to Air Law* [P,A] | 9th | Kluwer International | 2012 |
| Holding, John D. and Crush, Hon. Harvey | *The British Manual of International Air Carriage* [P] | | Irwin Law | 2009 |
| Leloudas, George | *Risk and Liability in Air Law* [P] | | Informa | 2009 |
| Philipson, Trevor, Q.C., *et al.* | *Carriage by Air* [P] | | Tottel | 2000 |
| Unmack, Tim | *Civil Aviation: Standards and Liabilities* [P] | | Informa | 1999 |

# ANIMAL LAW

A wide range of subtopics are included in this subject such as animal welfare and protection, veterinary surgeons, animals as property and the liability of the owners of animals. This is a largely statute-based subject area with such important statutes as *inter alia* the Animal Health Act 1981, Animal Welfare Act 2006, Dangerous Dogs Act 1991, and the Veterinary Surgeons Act 1966. There is however, a substantial body of case law especially as regards animal owner liability and game rights. There are also numerous European Union legislative provisions many dealing with the transportation of animals and protection of endangered species.

For sources dealing with farm animals, see AGRICULTURAL LAW.

*Related topic(s): AGRICULTURAL LAW; NUISANCE.*

| Author(s) | Title | Edition | Publisher | Year |
|---|---|---|---|---|
| McEldowney, John, Grant, Wyn, and Medley, Graham | *The Regulation of Animal Health and Welfare: Science, Law, and Policy* [A,P] | | Routledge | 2013 |
| MacKenzie, Julie | *Horse Law* [N] | 3rd | J.A. Allen & Co. Ltd. | 2012 |
| Clayden, Paul, ed. | *The Dog Law Handbook* [N] | 2nd | Sweet & Maxwell | 2011 |
| Dolan, Kevin | *Laboratory Animal Law: Legal Control of the Use of Animals in Research* [A,N] | 2nd | Wiley-Blackwell | 2007 |
| Gilligan, Brenda | *Practical Horse Law: A Guide for Owners and Riders* [N] | | Wiley-Blackwell | 2002 |
| Palmer, Julian | *Animal Law* [P,N] | 3rd | Shaw & Sons | 2001 |
| Radford, Mike | *Animal Welfare Law in Britain: Regulation and Responsibility* [A] | | Oxford University Press | 2001 |
| Brooman, Simon and Legge, Dr. Debbie | *Law Relating to Animals* [S] | | Routledge-Cavendish | 1997 |

## ARBITRATION and DISPUTE RESOLUTION

Arbitration is one of a series of alternatives to litigation which enables parties to solve legal disputes without recourse to a suit in a court of law. A broader term, alternative dispute resolution, does not normally include arbitration, but rather refers to such processes as conciliation, and mediation, and expert evaluation all of which are dealt with in the Civil Procedure Rules.

The basis of arbitration is statutory, specifically the Arbitration Act 1996, and numerous civil procedure rules and practice directives. In the area of international trade disputes the international convention, UNCITRAL (United Nations Commissions on International Trade Law) is foundational.

*Related topic(s): INTERNATIONAL TRADE LAW; INTERNATIONAL INVESTMENT LAW; LEGAL SKILLS and METHOD; PRACTICE & PROCEDURE (CIVIL).*

| Author(s) | Title | Edition | Publisher | Year |
|---|---|---|---|---|
| Merkin, Robert | *Arbitration Law* [P] | | Informa | LL |
| Blake, Susan, Browne, Julie, and Sime, Stuart | *The Jackson ADR Handbook* [P,A] | 2nd | Oxford University Press | 2016 |
| Walker, Stephen | *Mediation: An A-Z Guide* [S,N,P] | | Bloomsbury Professional | 2016 |
| Walker, Stephen | *Mediation Advocacy: Representing Clients in Mediation* [P,S] | | Bloomsbury Professional | 2015 |
| St. John Sutton, David, Gill, Judith, and Gearing, Matthew | *Russell on Arbitration* [P] | 24th | Sweet & Maxwell | 2015 |
| Blake, Susan, Browne, Julie, and Sime, Stuart | *A Practical Approach to Alternative Dispute Resolution* [P,S] | 3rd | Oxford University Press | 2014 |
| Harris, Bruce, Planterose, Rowan, and Tecks, Jonathan | *The Arbitration Act 1996: A Commentary* [P] | 5th | Wiley-Blackwell | 2014 |
| Merkin, Robert and Flannery, Louis | *Arbitration Act 1996* [P] | 5th | Informa | 2014 |

| | | | | |
|---|---|---|---|---|
| Brown, Henry and Marriott, Arthur, Q.C. | *ADR Principles and Practice* [P] | 3rd | Sweet & Maxwell | 2012 |
| Horn, Ben and Hopkins, Roger, eds. | *Arbitration Law Handbook* [P] | | Informa | 2007 |
| Tackaberry, John, Q.C. and Marriott, Arthur, Q.C. | *Bernstein's Handbook of Arbitration and Dispute Resolution Practice* [P] | 4th | Sweet & Maxwell | 2003 |

## Noteworthy websites, blogs, etc.:

### WEBSITE

- LexisNexis, Lexis Web: Dispute Resolution (http://lexisweb.co.uk/groups/dispute-resolution/default.aspx)

### BLOGS

- Paula Hodges, Laurence Shore, and Peter Godwin, Herbert Smith Freehills Arbitration Notes (http://hsfnotes.com/arbitration/)
- LexisNexis, Dispute Resolution Blog (http://blogs.lexisnexis.co.uk/dr/)
- Alexander Oddy, Peter Butler, and Julian Copeman, Herbert Smith Freehills ADR Notes (http://hsfnotes.com/adr/)

## BANKING and FINANCE LAW

The titles listed hereunder deal with the law as it relates to banks and other financial service providers, such as building societies. This is a mixed area of statute and case law. Prior to 2000 the principal enactment was the Banking Act 1987 however major portions of this were rolled into the Financial Services and Markets Act 2000 as the distinction between banking and other financial services was removed and these matters were brought under one legislative umbrella.

Other significant statutes are the Banking (Special Provisions) Act 2008 and the Banking Act 2009.

*Related topic(s): BILLS of EXCHANGE and LETTERS of CREDIT; SECURITIES.*

| **Author(s)** | **Title** | **Edition** | **Publisher** | **Year** |
|---|---|---|---|---|
| Burgess, Robert and Struan, Scott | *Law of Loans and Borrowing* [P] | | Sweet & Maxwell | LL |
| Cresswell, Sir Peter, *et. al.*, eds. | *Encyclopaedia of Banking Law* [P] | 2nd | LexisNexis Butterworths | LL |
| Brindle, Michael and Cox, Raymond, eds. | *Law of Bank Payments* [P] | 5th | Sweet & Maxwell | 2016 |
| Fuller, Geoffrey | *Corporate Borrowing: Law and Practice* [P] | 5th | Jordan Publishing | 2016 |
| Chiu, Iris H-Y | *Regulating (from) the Inside: The Legal Framework for Internal Controls in Banks and Financial Institutions* [P,A] | | Hart Publishing | 2015 |
| Proctor, Charles | *Law and Practice of International Banking* [P,A] | 2nd | Oxford University Press | 2015 |
| Sabalot, Deborah, ed. | *Butterworths Securities and Financial Services Law Handbook 2015* [P] | 12th | LexisNexis Butterworths | 2015* |
| Ferran, Eilis and Ho, Look Chan | *Principles of Corporate Finance Law* [S] | 2nd | Oxford University Press | 2014 |
| Malek, Ali Q.C. and Odgers, John, Q.C., eds. | *Paget's Law of Banking* [P] | 14th | LexisNexis Butterworths | 2014 |

| Author(s) | Title | Edition | Publisher | Year |
|---|---|---|---|---|
| Walker, George, Purves, Robert, and Blair, Michael, Q.C., eds. | *Financial Services Law* [P,A] | 3rd | Oxford University Press | 2014 |
| Hudson, Alastair | *The Law of Finance* [S,P,A] | 2nd | Sweet & Maxwell | 2013 |
| Ellinger, E.P., Lomnicka, E., and Hare, C.V.M. | *Ellinger's Modern Banking Law* [S,P] | 5th | Oxford University Press | 2011 |
| Blair, William and Maher, Felicity | *Butterworths Banking Law Handbook* [P] | 8th | LexisNexis Butterworths | 2010 |
| McCracken, Sheelagh | *The Banker's Remedy of Set-off* [P] | 3rd | Bloomsbury Professional | 2010 |
| Spangler, Timothy, ed. | *Investment Management Law and Practice* [P,A] | | Oxford University Press | 2010 |
| Blair, Michael, Q.C., ed. | *Blackstone's Guide to the Financial Services and Markets Act 2000* [P] | 2nd | Oxford University Press | 2009 |
| Benjamin, Joanna | *Financial Law* [P,A] | | Oxford University Press | 2007 |
| Munir, Abu Bakar | *Internet Banking: Law and Practice* [P] | | LexisNexis Butterworths | 2004 |
| Cranston, Ross | *Principles of Banking Law* [S] | 2nd | Oxford University Press | 2002 |

## Noteworthy websites, blogs, etc.:

### WEBSITES

- Fraud Advisory Panel, Resources (https://www.fraudadvisorypanel.org/resource/)
- LexisNexis, Lexis Web: Banking and Finance (http://lexisweb.co.uk/groups/banking-and-finance/default.aspx)
- LexisNexis, Lexis Web: Financial Services (http://lexisweb.co.uk/groups/financial-services/default.aspx)
- Herbert Smith Freehills (firm), Financial Services Regulation and Corporate Crime Notes (http://hsfnotes.com/fsrandcorpcrime/)

## BILLS of EXCHANGE and LETTERS of CREDIT

This particular area of law deals with methods of payment other than cash. Collectively these methods are called negotiable instruments and examples include cheques, promissory notes, bank notes, treasury bills, bonds, and postal orders. This area of law was one which long ago underwent codification by way of the Bills of Exchange Act 1882 which remains to this day the principal piece of legislation in the area.

*Related topic(s): BANKING and FINANCE LAW; COMMERCIAL LAW.*

| Author(s) | Title | Edition | Publisher | Year |
|---|---|---|---|---|
| Guest, A.G. | *Chalmers and Guest on Bills of Exchange, Cheques, and Promissory Notes* [P] | 18th | Sweet & Maxwell | 2016 |
| Elliott, Nicholas, Odgers, John, and Phillips, Jonathan Mark | *Byles on Bills of Exchange and Cheques* [P] | 29th | Sweet & Maxwell | 2013 |
| Ellinger, Peter and Neo, Dora | *The Law and Practice of Documentary Letters of Credit* [P] | | Hart Publishing | 2010 |
| Horowitz, Deborah | *Letters of Credit and Demand Guarantees: Defences to Payment* [P] | | Oxford University Press | 2010 |
| Malek, Ali Q.C. and Quest, David | *Jack: Documentary Credits* [P] | 4th | Tottel | 2009 |
| Hedley, William and Hedley, Richard | *Bills of Exchange and Bankers' Documentary Credits* [P] | 4th | Informa | 2001 |

# CHARITIES

This topic deals with the law of charitable organisations, i.e., institutions which have been established exclusively for a charitable purpose. Needless to say, much of the legal activity associated with this subject deals with the determination of whether or not an organisation's activities are, in fact, charitable.

Other important sub-topics in the law of charities include charitable trusts and the cy-près doctrine, and charitable corporations.

The most influential statute in play is the Charities Act 2006, which establishes criteria for designation as a charity and establishes the Charity Tribunal. Another noteworthy statute is the Trustee Act 2000.

*Related topic(s): COMPANY LAW; TRUSTS.*

| Author(s) | Title | Edition | Publisher | Year |
|---|---|---|---|---|
| Cracknell, Douglas, *et al.*, eds. | *Charities: The Law and Practice* [P] | | Sweet & Maxwell | LL |
| Alexander, Con, *et al.*, eds. | *Jordan's Charities Administration* [P] | | Jordan Publishing | LL |
| Mazars LLP and Withers LLP | *Tolley's Charities Manual* [P] | | LexisNexis Butterworths | LL |
| Blake, Julian and Walker, Alice Faure | *Charities Act Handbook: A Practical Guide to the Charities Act* [P] | | Jordan Publishing | 2015 |
| Henderson, William, Fowles, Jonathan, and Smith, Julian | *Tudor on Charities* [P] | 10th | Sweet & Maxwell | 2015 |
| Alexander, Con, *et al.* | *Charities Governance* [P] | 2nd | Jordan Publishing | 2014 |
| Gillard, Cecile | *Charities and Not-for-Profit Entities: Law and Practice* [P] | | Wildy Simmonds & Hill | 2012 |
| Picarda, Hubert, Q.C. | *The Law and Practice Relating to Charities* [P] | 4th | Bloomsbury Professional | 2010 |
| Lloyd, Stephen and Walker, Alice Faure | *Charities, Trading and the Law* [P] | 2nd | Jordan Publishing | 2009 |

| | | | | |
|---|---|---|---|---|
| Meakin, Robert | *The Law of Charitable Status: Maintenance and Removal* [P] | | Cambridge University Press | 2008 |

# CHILDREN

The titles listed hereunder deal with children and the law in all contexts other than that of custody and access, titles for which are listed under FAMILY LAW. The topics dealt with in the works below include the legal status of children, adoption, foster children, financial support of children (maintenance), employment of children, children and youths and criminal proceedings, parentage, surrogacy, youth and anti-social behaviour, governmental requirements of childminders, among numerous other matters.

A substantial number of statutes deal specifically with matters related to children including the Children Act 1989, Children Act 2004, Adoption and Children Act 2002, Child Support Act 1991, Childcare Act 2006, and Youth Justice and Criminal Evidence Act 1999. There are also relevant European Union regulations.

*Related topic(s): CRIMINAL LAW; FAMILY LAW; POLICE and PUBLIC ORDER LAW; PRACTICE & PROCEDURE (CIVIL); PRACTICE & PROCEDURE (CRIMINAL); SOCIAL SECURITY and WELFARE LAW.*

| Author(s) | Title | Edition | Publisher | Year |
|---|---|---|---|---|
| Hershman, David, McFarlane, Andrew | *Children Law and Practice* [P] | | Family Law | LL |
| Jones, Richard M, ed. | *Encyclopedia of Social Services and Child Care Law* [P] | | Sweet & Maxwell | LL |
| Lowe, Nigel *et al.* | *Clarke Hall and Morrison on Children* [P] | | LexisNexis Butterworths | LL |
| Hershman, David and McFarlane, Andrew | *Children Act Handbook 2015/16* [P] | | Jordan Publishing | 2015* |
| Jacobs, Edward | *Child Support: The Legislation* [P] | 12th | Child Poverty Action Group | 2015* |
| Broach, Stephen, Clements, Luke, and Read, Janet | *Disabled Children: A Legal Handbook* [P] | 2nd | Legal Action Group | 2015 |
| The Law Society | *Good Practice in Child Care Cases: A Guide for Solicitors Acting in Public Law Children Act Proceedings* [P] | 3rd | The Law Society | 2015 |
| Arnold, Noel | *Children and Families Act 2014: Family Justice Under the New Law* [P] | | The Law Society | 2014 |

| Author(s) | Title | Edition | Publisher | Year |
|---|---|---|---|---|
| Bainham, Andrew and Gilmore, Stephen | *Children: The Modern Law* [P,S] | 4th | Family Law | 2013 |
| Bridgeman, Jo | *Parental Responsibility, Young Children, and Healthcare Law* [A] | | Cambridge University Press | 2012 |
| Isaacs, Elizabeth and Shepherd, Carmel | *Social Work decision-making: a Guide for Childcare Lawyers* [P,N] | 2nd | Family Law | 2012 |
| Mitchell, Hon. Judge John | *Children Act Private Law Proceedings: a Handbook* [P] | 3rd | Family Law | 2012 |
| Mitchels, Barbara, *et al.* | *Child Care and Protection: the Law and Practice* [P,S] | 5th | Wildy Simmonds & Hill | 2012 |
| Macdonald, Alistair | *The Rights of the Child: Law and Practice* [P,A] | | Jordan Publishing | 2011 |
| Hoyano, Laura and Keenan, Caroline | *Child Abuse Law and Policy across Boundaries* [A,P] | | Oxford University Press | 2010 |
| McFarlane, Andrew and Reardon, Madeleine | *Child Care and Adoption Law: A Practical Guide* [P] | 2nd | Jordan Publishing | 2010 |
| Bird, Roger and Burrows, David | *Child Maintenance: The New Law* [P] | | Jordan Publishing | 2009 |
| Pressdee, Piers, *et. al.* | *Contact: the New Deal* [P] | | Jordan Publishing | 2006 |
| Engelman, Philip and Spencer, Paul | *Blackstone's Guide to the Care Standards Act 2000* [P] | | Oxford University Press | 2003 |

## Noteworthy websites, blogs, etc.:

### BLOG

- Diane Benussi, Family Law Blog (http://www.benussilaw.co.uk/category/family-law-blog/)

# COMMERCIAL LAW

The heading 'commercial law' (interchangeable with the term 'business law') is used as a category under which titles dealing with the law as it relates to carrying on a business or commercial enterprise are listed. As such it is something of an umbrella term comprising numerous other legal topics. The titles listed here will deal with most or all of the following: contracts, property, agency, sale of goods, consumer law, intellectual property, bills of exchange, banking and finance, insurance, securities, international trade law, and commercial dispute resolution.

*Related topic(s): ACCOUNTING LAW; AGENCY; BANKING and FINANCE LAW; BILLS of EXCHANGE and LETTERS of CREDIT; COMPANY LAW; COMPETITION LAW; CONSUMER LAW; CONTRACT LAW; DATA PROTECTION; DEBTOR & CREDITOR LAW; EMPLOYMENT and LABOUR LAW; FRANCHISING LAW; HEALTH AND SAFETY; INFORMATION TECHNOLOGY LAW; INSURANCE LAW; INTELLECTUAL PROPERTY LAW; INTERNATIONAL TRADE LAW; PARTNERSHIP LAW; PATENTS; PROPERTY LAW; SALE of GOODS; TORT LAW; TRADE MARKS.*

| Author(s) | Title | Edition | Publisher | Year |
|---|---|---|---|---|
| Devenney, James, Johnson, Howard, and Paul Wragg | *Text, Cases and Materials on Commercial Law* [A,S] | | Routledge | 2016 |
| Dobson, Paul and Stokes, Rob | *Commercial Law Textbook* [S] | 9th | Sweet & Maxwell | 2016 |
| McKendrick, Ewan, Goode, Roy, eds. | *Goode on Commercial Law* [P,A,S] | 5th | LexisNexis Butterworths | 2016 |
| Burrows, Andrew, ed. | *Principles of English Commercial Law* [A,S,P] | | Oxford University Press | 2015 |
| Mawrey, Richard B. and Riley-Smith, Tobias, eds. | *Butterworths Commercial and Consumer Law Handbook* [P] | 8th | LexisNexis Butterworths | 2015 |
| Rose, Francis, ed. | *Blackstone's Statutes on Commercial & Consumer Law 2015-16* [P,S] | | Oxford University Press | 2015 |
| Baskind, Eric, Osborne, Greg, and Lee, Roach | *Commercial Law* [A,S] | | Oxford University Press | 2013 |

| | | | | |
|---|---|---|---|---|
| Furmston, Michael and Chuah, Jason, eds. | *Commercial Law* [S] | 2nd | Pearson Education | 2013 |
| Riches, Sarah and Allen, Vida | *Keenan & Riches' Business Law* [S] | 11th | Pearson Education | 2013 |
| Cakebread, Stuart | *Drafting Commercial Agreements* [P] | | The Law Society | 2010 |
| Berry, David, ed. | *Commercial Law Handbook* [P] | | The Law Society | 2009 |
| Sealy, Len S. and Hooley, Richard | *Commercial Law: Text, Cases, and Materials* [S] | 4th | Oxford University Press | 2008 |

## Noteworthy websites, blogs, etc.:

### WEBSITE

- Carruthers Law (firm), (http://www.carruthers-law.co.uk/news-articles/#.Vs8iyZwrK71)
- Fraud Advisory Panel, Resources (https://www.fraudadvisorypanel.org/resource/)
- LexisNexis, Lexis Web: Commercial (http://lexisweb.co.uk/groups/commercial/default.aspx)

# COMPANY LAW

Although not all companies are by definition incorporated, in England the term 'company law' normally refers to companies which in fact have been incorporated by way of registration pursuant to the Companies Act 2006. Referred to as 'corporate law' in other jurisdictions, company law is a particularly complex area of law dating back numerous centuries. Its fundamentals are grounded in a huge body of jurisprudence and in the Companies Act 2006.

Sub-topics particular to company law include directors' duties and liabilities, the powers and liabilities of companies, the requirements of reporting and publishing annual reports, share capital, securities, insider dealing, *inter alia.*

*Related topic(s): ACCOUNTING LAW; BANKING and FINANCE LAW; COMMERCIAL LAW; COMPETITION LAW; INTERNATIONAL INVESTMENT LAW; PARTNERSHIP LAW; SECURITIES.*

| **Author(s)** | **Title** | **Edition** | **Publisher** | **Year** |
|---|---|---|---|---|
| Millett, The Rt Hon the Lord, *et al.* | *Gore-Browne on Companies* [P] | 45th | Jordan Publishing | LL |
| Morse, Geoffrey | *Palmer's Company Law* [P] | | Sweet & Maxwell | LL |
| French, Derek, ed. | *Blackstone's Statutes on Company Law 2015-16* [P,S] | | Oxford University Press | Annual |
| Walmsley, Keith | *Butterworths Company Law Handbook* [P] | 29th | LexisNexis Butterworths | Annual |
| Wareham, Robert and Dolton, Alan | *Tolley's Company Law Handbook* [P] | | LexisNexis Butterworths | Annual |
| Hannigan, Brenda M. | *Company Law* [S] | 4th | Oxford University Press | 2015 |
| Joffe, Victor, Drake, David, Richardson, Giles, and Lightman, Daniel | *Minority Shareholders: Law, Practice and Procedure* [P] | 5th | Oxford University Press | 2015 |
| McLaughlin, Susan | *Unlocking Company Law* [S] | 3rd | Routledge | 2015 |
| Birds, John, *et al.*, eds. | *Boyle & Birds' Company Law* [A,P,S] | 9th | Jordan Publishing | 2014 |

| Author(s) | Title | Edition | Publisher | Year |
|---|---|---|---|---|
| Dine, Janet and Koutsias, Marios | *Palgrave Law Masters: Company Law* [P,S] | 8th | Palgrave Macmillan | 2014 |
| Hollington, Robin | *Shareholders' Rights* [P] | 7th | Sweet & Maxwell | 2013 |
| Mortimore, Simon, Q.C., ed. | *Company Directors: Duties, Liabilities and Remedies* [P] | 2nd | Oxford University Press | 2013 |
| Davies, Paul L. | *Gower and Davies' Principles of Modern Company Law* [S,P,A] | 9th | Sweet & Maxwell | 2012 |
| Lowry, John, Reisberg, Arad, and Pettet, Ben, | *Pettet's Company Law: Company and Corporate Finance* [S] | 4th | Pearson Education | 2012 |
| Bennett, David A., *et al.* | *Palmer's Company Law: Annotated Guide to the Companies Act 2006* [P] | 2nd | Sweet & Maxwell | 2009 |
| Hannigan, Brenda M. and Prentice, Dan | *The Companies Act 2006—A Commentary* [P] | 2nd | LexisNexis Butterworths | 2009 |

## Noteworthy websites, blogs, etc.:

### WEBSITES

- LexisNexis, Lexis Web: Commercial (http://lexisweb.co.uk/groups/commercial/default.aspx)
- LexisNexis, Lexis Web: Company Commercial (http://lexisweb.co.uk/groups/company-commercial/default.aspx)
- LexisNexis, Lexis Web: Corporate (http://lexisweb.co.uk/groups/corporate/default.aspx)

### BLOG

- Robert Goddard, Corporate Law and Governance (http://www.corporatelawandgovernance.blogspot.co.uk/)

# COMPARATIVE LAW

Comparative law is the study and comparison of different legal systems throughout the world. Major systems include the common law of the "legal Anglosphere", the civil law system from continental Europe, Islamic law, and socialist legal systems. There are also jurisdictions with mixed systems, an obvious example of which is the United Kingdom in so far as Scotland has a civil law basis to components of its law. Canada is a bijural country with the province of Quebec employing a civil law system for its private law as does the state of Louisiana in the United. Numerous countries' legal systems are blends of different systems, such as India whose system is an amalgam of civil, common, and religious law. Listed below are comparative law titles of English origin.

| Author(s) | Title | Edition | Publisher | Year |
|---|---|---|---|---|
| Bussani, Mauro and Sebok, Anthony, eds. | *Comparative Tort Law: Global Perspectives* [A] | | Edward Elgar | 2015 |
| Gutteridge, Harold C. | *Comparative Law: An Introduction to the Comparative Method of Legal Study and Research* [A] | | Cambridge University Press | 2015 |
| Wilcox, Russell, *et al.*, eds. | *Journal of Comparative Law Studies in Comparative Law* (14 vols.) [A] | | Wildy, Simmonds & Hill | 2015 |
| Andenas, Mads and Fairgrieve, Duncan | *Courts and Comparative Law* [A] | | Oxford University Press | 2015 |
| Farran, Sue, Orucu, Esin, and Donlan, Sean Patrick, eds. | *A Study of Mixed Legal Systems: Endangered, Entrenched or Blended* [A] | | Ashgate | 2014 |
| Rosenfeld, Michel and Sajo, Andras, eds. | *The Oxford Handbook of Comparative Constitutional Law* [A,S] | | Oxford University Press | 2012 |
| Bingham of Cornhill, Baron | *Widening Horizons: The Influence of Comparative Law and International Law on Domestic Law* [A] | | Cambridge University Press | 2010 |
| Orucu, Esin | *Mixed Legal Systems at New Frontiers* [A] | | Wildy, Simmonds & Hill | 2010 |

| Author(s) | Title | Edition | Publisher | Year |
|---|---|---|---|---|
| Gordley, James and Taylor von Mehren, Arthur | *An Introduction to the Comparative Study of Private Law: Readings, Cases, Materials* [A] | | Cambridge University Press | 2009 |
| Markesinis, Basil and Fedtke, Joerg | *Engaging with Foreign Law* [A] | | Hart | 2009 |
| Reimann, Mathias and Zimmermann, Reinhard | *The Oxford Handbook of Comparative Law* [A] | | Oxford University Press | 2008 |
| Canivet, Guy, Andenas, Mads, and Fairgrieve, Duncan, eds. | *Comparative Law Before the Courts* [A] | | British Institute of International and Comparative Law | 2004 |

# COMPETITION LAW

The term 'competition law' refers to an array of activities intended to provide protection from unfair or inefficient competition. These activities are accomplished largely through the application of statutes, statutory instruments, and European regulations. There is also a sizable body of case law applicable to these topics.

Specific practices which competition law attempts to address include mergers, monopolies, and fair trading. There are two principal statutes which shape this area of law: the Enterprise and Regulatory Reform Act 2013 and the Competition Act 1998, the former of which deals primarily with mergers and enables market investigations. The latter statute focuses on practices which distort competition or abuse a trader's dominant market position. The Enterprise and Regulatory Reform Act 2013 established the Competition and Markets Authority (CMA) which has a wide range of powers to promote competitive practices and restrict those which threaten competitiveness and efficiency. It also provides the enforcement mechanism against practices which are contrary to the European Union's prohibitions against activities which prevent, restrict or distort competition or which abuse a competitor's dominant position. The CMA has assumed the roles of the Competition Commission and the Office of Fair Trading resulting in the abolishment of those agencies.

It is worth noting that the European Union began as a common trade market and as such the treaty which established the European Community comprises numerous articles which deal with trade provisions and prohibitions against anti-competitive trading.

*Related topic(s): COMMERCIAL LAW; EUROPEAN UNION LAW; SALE of GOODS.*

| **Author(s)** | **Title** | **Edition** | **Publisher** | **Year** |
|---|---|---|---|---|
| | *Encyclopedia of Competition Law* [P] | | Sweet & Maxwell | LL |
| Whish, Richard, *et al.* | *Butterworths Competition Law Service* [P] | | LexisNexis Butterworths | LL |
| Bavasso, Antonio, ed. | *Butterworths Competition Law Handbook* [P] | 21st | LexisNexis Butterworths | Annual |
| Korah, Valentine | *Competition Law: Text, Cases and Materials* [A,S] | 4th | Hart | 2016 |

| Author(s) | Title | Edition | Publisher | Year |
|---|---|---|---|---|
| Rose, Vivien and Bailey, David | *Bellamy & Child: European Union Law of Competition* [P,S] | 7th | Oxford University Press | 2015* |
| Whish, Richard and Bailey, David | *Competition Law* [S,P] | 8th | Oxford University Press | 2015 |
| Faull, Jonathan and Nikpay, Ali | *The EU Law of Competition* [P,A] | 3rd | Oxford University Press | 2014 |
| Carrier, Michael, ed. | *Intellectual Property and Competition* [A,P] | | Edward Elgar | 2011 |
| Wadlow, Christopher | *The Law of Passing-Off: Unfair Competition by Misrepresentation* [P] | 4th | Sweet & Maxwell | 2011 |
| Goyder, Joanna and Albors-Llorens, Albertina | *Goyder's EC Competition Law* [S] | 5th | Oxford University Press | 2009 |
| Van Bael, Ivo and Bellis, Jean-Francois | *Competition Law of the European Community* [P,A] | 5th | Wolters Kluwer | 2009 |
| Korah, Valentine | *An Introductory Guide to EC Competition Law and Practice* [S] | 9th | Hart | 2007 |
| O'Neill, Elizabeth and Scaife, Emma | *UK Competition Procedure: The Modernised Regime* [P] | | Oxford University Press | 2007 |

## Noteworthy websites, blogs, etc.:

### WEBSITES

- Jordan Publishing, Jordan's Competition Law Online (http://www.jordanpublishing.co.uk/practice-areas/competition)
- LexisNexis, Lexis Web: Competition (http://lexisweb.co.uk/groups/competition/default.aspx)

# CONFLICT of LAWS

Also referred to as "private international law" this term applies to matters which in some way have a connection to a foreign jurisdiction and the issue arises as to which jurisdiction provides an appropriate venue for resolving the dispute. Most countries have domestic law which assists courts in making the above determinations. There is even a legal concept called, *renvoi*, by which English courts can, in specific circumstances, apply the domestic law of the foreign jurisdiction.

Common topics which frequently arise in conflict of laws disputes include family law and maintenance matters, insolvency, successions law, and contracts.

There is a body of statutes which deal with foreign judgments and their enforcement in the United Kingdom. Examples include Foreign Corporations Act 1991, Foreign Judgments (Reciprocal Enforcement) Act 1933, Foreign Marriage Act 1892, Maintenance Orders (Reciprocal Enforcement) Act 1972, and Private International Law (Miscellaneous Provisions) Act 1995.

There are also numerous international treaties and conventions which mandate the enforcement of one jurisdiction's decisions in another. Examples are the Brussels, Rome, and Lugano Conventions. The Rome I and Rome II regulations deal with choice of law in civil and commercial litigation related to certain obligations.

*Related topic(s): INTERNATIONAL CRIMINAL LAW; INTERNATIONAL LAW; INTERNATIONAL INVESTMENT LAW; INTERNATIONAL TRADE LAW.*

| Author(s) | Title | Edition | Publisher | Year |
|---|---|---|---|---|
| Briggs, Adrian | *Civil Jurisdiction and Judgments* [P,S] | 6th | Informa Law | 2015 |
| Lord Collins of Mapesbury, *et al.*, eds. | *Dicey, Morris and Collins on the Conflict of Laws* [P,A] | 15th | Sweet & Maxwell | 2015* |
| George, Martin and Dickinson, Andrew, eds. | *Statutes on the Conflict of Laws* [S] | | Hart | 2015 |
| Joseph, David | *Jurisdiction and Arbitration Agreements and their Enforcement* [P] | 3rd | Sweet & Maxwell | 2015 |
| Plender, Richard and Wilderspin, Michael | *The European Private International Law of Obligations* [A,P] | 4th | Sweet & Maxwell | 2014 |
| Briggs, Adrian | *The Conflict of Laws* [S] | 3rd | Oxford University Press | 2013 |

| Author(s) | Title | Edition | Publisher | Year |
|---|---|---|---|---|
| Harding, Maebh | *Conflict of Laws* [P,S] | 5th | Routledge-Cavendish | 2013 |
| McClean, David and Abou-Nigm, Veronica Ruiz | *Morris: The Conflict of Laws* [S,P,A] | 8th | Sweet & Maxwell | 2012 |
| Clarkson, C.M.V. and Hill, Jonathan | *The Conflict of Laws* [P] | 4th | Oxford University Press | 2011 |
| Briggs, Adrian | *Agreements on Jurisdiction and Choice of Law* [P,A] | | Oxford University Press | 2008 |
| Fawcett, James, Carruthers, Janeen, and North, Sir Peter | *Cheshire, North, & Fawcett: Private International Law* [S,P] | 14th | Oxford University Press | 2008 |
| Hood, Kirsty J. | *Conflict of Laws within the UK* [P,A] | | Oxford University Press | 2007 |

## Noteworthy websites, blogs, etc.:

### WEBSITE

- Journal of Private International Law, Conflict of Laws.net (http://conflictoflaws.net/)

# CONSTITUTIONAL LAW

For the purposes of this listing, 'Constitutional Law' refers to the organisation of the state's governing apparatus and the manner in which it interacts with its citizenry.

In the absence of a specifically articulated written document, the United Kingdom's constitution is comprised of myriad customs, doctrines, jurisprudence, statutory provisions, and codes of conduct which have evolved over more than a millennium. This makes it a more flexible, fluid area of law than is often the case in states with a written constitution.

The most profound single change to the country's constitution occurred in 1973 with the United Kingdom's entry into the European Community. Prior to this date a fundamental constitutional concept had long been the supremacy of Parliament. Since admission to the European Community, however, all Parliamentary enactments must be in accord with European Union law bringing Parliamentary primacy into question.

Notable recent changes have been made by way of statute. For example, the creation of the Supreme Court of the United Kingdom was done so by way of the Constitutional Reform Act 2005. This act also made changes to the powers of the Judicial Committee of the Privy Council. Less significant constitutional reform was made by the Constitutional Reform and Governance Act 2010 which deals with rules for entering into international treaties and which affects the Royal Prerogative (the ability of the monarch [or more commonly the cabinet] to act without Parliamentary approval).

For the manner in which the individual engages in legal disputes with the state, see ADMINISTRATIVE LAW. For constitutionally defined human rights, see DISCRIMINATION LAW and HUMAN RIGHTS and CIVIL LIBERTIES.

*Related topic(s): ADMINISTRATIVE LAW; CROWN LAW; DISCRIMINATION LAW; ENGLISH LEGAL SYSTEM; EUROPEAN UNION LAW; HUMAN RIGHTS and CIVIL LIBERTIES; LOCAL GOVERNMENT LAW.*

| Author(s) | Title | Edition | Publisher | Year |
|---|---|---|---|---|
| Barnett, Hilaire | *Constitutional & Administrative Law* [S] | 11th | Routledge | 2015 |
| Loveland, Ian | Constitutional Law, Administrative Law, and Human Rights: A Critical Introduction [S,A] | 7th | Oxford University Press | 2015 |

| Author(s) | Title | Edition | Publisher | Year |
|---|---|---|---|---|
| Webley, Lisa and Samuels, Harriet | *Complete Public Law: Text, Cases, and Materials* [S] | 3rd | Oxford University Press | 2015 |
| Bradley, A.W., Ewing, K.D., and Knight, Christopher | *Constitutional and Administrative Law* [S] | 16th | Pearson Education | 2014 |
| Parpworth, Neil | *Core Text: Constitutional & Administrative Law* [S] | 8th | Oxford University Press | 2014 |
| Ryan, Mark and Foster, Steve | *Unlocking Constitutional & Administrative Law* [S] | 3rd | Hodder Education | 2014 |
| Allison, J.W.F. ed. | *Dicey: The Law of the Constitution* (vol. 1); *Comparative Constitutionalism* (vol. 2) [A,P,S] | | Oxford University Press | 2013 |
| Le Sueur, Andrew, Sunkin, Maurice, and Murkens, Jo | *Public Law: Text, Cases, and Materials* [S] | 2nd | Oxford University Press | 2013 |
| Jack, Malcolm, ed. | *Erskine May Parliamentary Practice* [P] | 24th | LexisNexis Butterworth | 2011 |
| Feldman, David | *English Public Law* [P,A] | 2nd | Oxford University Press | 2009 |
| King, Anthony | *The British Constitution* [S] | | Oxford University Press | 2009 |
| Giussani, Elizabeth | *Constitutional & Administrative Law* [A,P] | | Sweet & Maxwell | 2008 |

## Noteworthy websites, blogs, etc.:

### WEBSITES

- Jordan Publishing, Public Law and Regulation: Case Reports (http://www.jordanpublishing.co.uk/practice-areas/public-law/news_and_comment?filter[category_id]=2433)

### BLOGS

- London School of Economics and Political Science, Constitution UK (http://blogs.lse.ac.uk/constitutionuk/)
- UK Administrative Justice Institute, Blog (https://ukaji.org/)

# CONSTRUCTION LAW

Construction law (which is also sometimes referred to as 'building law') deals with all manner of legal issues related to the construction of buildings and edifices. Aspects of this topic fall within the public law sphere, e.g., adherence to building regulations and planning, but most are private law matters, particularly contractual issues, negligence, and nuisance.

The primary statute in England related to buildings is the Building Act 1984.

*Related topic(s): DESIGNS; LOCAL GOVERNMENT LAW; NEGLIGENCE; NUISANCE; PLANNING LAW; PROFESSIONAL NEGLIGENCE.*

| Author(s) | Title | Edition | Publisher | Year |
|---|---|---|---|---|
| Levine, Marshall | *Construction and Engineering Precedents* [P] | | Sweet & Maxwell | LL |
| Lloyd, His Honour Judge Humphrey and Bartlett, Andrew | *Emden's Construction Law* [P] | | LexisNexis Butterworths | LL |
| Chern, Cyril | *The Law of Construction Disputes* [P] | 2nd | Informa | 2016 |
| Burr, Andrew | *Delay and Disruption In Construction Contracts* [P] | 5th | Informa | 2016 |
| Coulson, Peter | *Coulson on Construction Adjudication* [P] | 3rd | Oxford University Press | 2015 |
| Dennys, Nicholas, Raeside, Mark, and Clay, Robert, eds. | *Hudson's Building and Engineering Contracts* [P] | 13th | Sweet & Maxwell | 2015* |
| Pickavance, James | *A Practical Guide to Construction Adjudication* [P] | | Wiley-Blackwell | 2015 |
| Royce, Darryl | *Adjudication in Construction Law*[P] | | Informa | 2015 |
| Wilmot-Smith, Richard, Q.C. | *Wilmot-Smith on Construction Contracts* [P] | 3rd | Oxford University Press | 2014 |
| Uff, John | *Construction Law* [S] | 11th | Sweet & Maxwell | 2013 |
| Furst, Stephen and Ramsay, the Hon. Sir Vivian | *Keating on Construction Contracts* [P] | 9th | Sweet & Maxwell | 2012* |
| Adriaanse, John | *Construction Contract Law: The Essentials* [S] | 3rd | Palgrave MacMillan | 2010 |

| Author(s) | Title | Edition | Publisher | Year |
|---|---|---|---|---|
| Speaight, Anthony and Stone, Gregory | *Architect's Legal Handbook: The Law for Architects* [N,P] 🖱 | 9th | Architectural Press | 2010 |
| ter Haar, Roger and ter Haar, Camilla | *Remedies in Construction Law* [P] 🖱 | | Informa | 2010 |
| Barrett, Kevin | *Defective Construction Work* [P] | | Blackwell | 2008 |

## Noteworthy websites, blogs, etc.:

### WEBSITE

- LexisNexis, Lexis Web: Construction (http://lexisweb.co.uk/groups/construction/default.aspx)

### BLOG

- LexisNexis, Purpose Built Blog (http://blogs.lexisnexis.co.uk/purposebuilt/)

# CONSUMER LAW

Also called 'consumer protection law' this area has developed over recent decades, although some provisions, such as those related to weights and measures date back centuries. Consumer law is often viewed as a subset of sale of goods but the titles listed here extend out more broadly to include, for example, product liability which is a specific branch of tort law. Another important component of consumer law deals with consumer credit which is governed largely by the Consumer Credit Act 1974 and the Consumer Credit Act 2006 the latter of which created the Financial Ombudsman Service through which consumers can seek to resolve a dispute with a creditor.

Other relevant statutes include: the Consumer Protection Act 1987, Trade Descriptions Act 1968, and the Sale of Goods Act 1979. There is also an overlay of European Union law through certain statutory provisions.

*Related topic(s): DEBTOR & CREDITOR; NEGLIGENCE; SALE of GOODS; TORT LAW.*

| Author(s) | Title | Edition | Publisher | Year |
|---|---|---|---|---|
| Miller, C.J., *et al.* | *Product Liability and Safety Encyclopaedia* [P] | | LexisNexis Butterworths | LL |
| Parry, Deborah L. and Rowell, Roland | *Butterworths Trading and Consumer Law* [P] | | LexisNexis Butterworths | LL |
| Fairgrieve, Duncan and Goldberg, R.S. | *Product Liability* [P,A] | 3rd | Oxford University Press | 2016 |
| Andrews, Claire | *Enforcement of Consumer Protection Legislation: Law and Practice* [P] | | LexisNexis Butterworths | 2015 |
| Lewin, Bryan and Kirk, Jonathan | *Consumer and Trading Standards: Law and Practice* [P] | 4th | Jordan | 2015 |
| Mawrey, Richard B. and Riley-Smith, Tobias, eds. | *Butterworths Commercial and Consumer Law Hand-book* [P] | 8th | LexisNexis Butterworths | 2015 |
| Downes, John and Paton, Tricia | *Travel and Tourism Law in the UK* [N] | 5th | Elm Publications | 2011 |
| Furmston, Michael and Chuah, Jason, eds. | *Commercial Law* [S] | | Pearson Education | 2013 |

| Author(s) | Title | Edition | Publisher | Year |
|---|---|---|---|---|
| Rosenthal, Dennis | *Consumer Credit Law and Practice: A Guide* [P] | 4th | Bloomsbury Professional | 2013 |
| Woodroffe, Geoffrey and Lowe, Robert | *Woodroffe and Lowe's Consumer Law and Practice* [S,P] | 9th | Sweet & Maxwell | 2013 |
| Philpott, Fred, *et al.* | *The Law of Consumer Credit and Hire* [P,A] | | Oxford University Press | 2009 |
| Howells, Geraint, ed. | *Law of Product Liability* [P,A] | 2nd | LexisNexis Butterworths | 2007 |
| Howells, Geraint and Weatherill, Stephen | *Consumer Protection Law* [A,P] | 2nd | Ashgate | 2005 |

# CONTRACT LAW

Contract law is one of oldest branches of English law. Its authority comes almost entirely from the common law (with a few equitable remedies added in) and it sometimes strays into the area of tort law. A contract is in essence an agreement or promise which is enforceable at law. Simple as that concept might be, contract law is a particularly complex legal area which has developed over many centuries. Frequently researched contract principles include the formation of the contract (e.g., what constitutes offer and acceptance), the effects of undue influence on a party, privity of contract (i.e., the parties to the contract), consideration, mistake, rescission (bringing the contract to an end), and void or illegal contracts.

As the fundamentals of contract law have their basis in case law, there are few relevant statutes. However, three to note are the Misrepresentation Act 1967, the Sale of Goods Act 1979, and the Unfair Contract Terms Act 1977.

As a contract is a common legal instrument used in a variety undertakings it is given treatment in works listed under numerous other topics.

*Related topic(s): AGENCY; BANKING and FINANCE LAW; BILLS of EXCHANGE and LETTERS of CREDIT; COMMERCIAL LAW; COMPANY LAW; CONSTRUCTION LAW; CONSUMER LAW; DEBTOR & CREDITOR LAW; DRAFTING and LEGAL WRITING; EMPLOYMENT and LABOUR LAW; EQUITY & TRUSTS; FAMILY LAW; FRANCHISING LAW; FRAUD and MISPREPRESENTATION; INSURANCE LAW; LOANS and MORTGAGES; PARTNERSHIP LAW; PENSIONS LAW; PROPERTY LAW; REAL PROPERTY; REMEDIES, DAMAGES, and RESITUTION; SALE of GOODS; TORT LAW.*

| Author(s) | Title | Edition | Publisher | Year |
|---|---|---|---|---|
| Singleton, Susan | *E-Contracts* [P] | | Bloomsbury Professional | LL |
| Feltham, Piers, *et al.* | *Spencer Bower on the Law Relating to Estoppel by Representation* [P,A] | 5th | Bloomsbury Professional | 2016 |
| Furmston, Michael and Tolhurst, G.J. | *Privity of Contract* [P,A] | | Oxford University Press | 2015 |
| Beale, Hugh | *Chitty on Contracts* [P,A] | 32nd | Sweet & Maxwell | 2015* |
| Lewison, Kim | *The Interpretation of Contracts* [P,A] | 6th | Sweet & Maxwell | 2015* |
| Nwakado, Rex | *Tolley's Commercial Contracts, Transactions and Precedents* [P] | 2nd | LexisNexis Butterworths | 2015 |

| Author(s) | Title | Edition | Publisher | Year |
|---|---|---|---|---|
| Peel, Edwin | *Treitel: The Law of Contract* [S,P,A] | 14th | Sweet & Maxwell | 2015 |
| Rose, Francis, ed. | *Blackstone's Statutes on Contracts, Tort & Restitution 2015-16* [P,S] | | Oxford University Press | 2015* |
| Stone, Richard and Devenney, James | *The Modern Law of Contract* [S,A] | 11th | Routledge | 2015 |
| Kramer, Adam | *The Law of Contract Damages* [P,A] | | Hart | 2014 |
| Lawson, Richard | *Exclusion Clauses and Unfair Contract Terms* [P] | 11th | Sweet & Maxwell | 2014 |
| Murray, Ryan | *Contract Law: The Fundamentals* [S] | 3rd | Sweet & Maxwell | 2014 |
| O'Sullivan, Dominic, Elliott, Steven, and Zakrzewski, Rafal | *The Law of Rescission* [P,A] | 2nd | Oxford University Press | 2014 |
| Furmston, Michael | *Cheshire, Fifoot, and Furmston's Law of Contract* [S,P] | 16th | Oxford University Press | 2012 |
| McMeel, Gerard | *The Construction of Contracts: Interpretation, Implication, and Rectification* [P,A] | 2nd | Oxford University Press | 2011 |
| Beatson, J., Burrows, A., and Cartwright, J. | *Anson's Law of Contract* [S,A,P] | 29th | Oxford University Press | 2010 |
| Furmston, Michael | *The Law of Contract* [S] | 4th | LexisNexis Butterworths | 2010 |
| Upex, Robert and Bennett, Geoffrey | *Davies on Contract* [S] | 10th | Sweet & Maxwell | 2008 |
| Mitchell, Charles and Watterson, Stephen | *Subrogation: Law and Practice* [P,A] | | Oxford University Press | 2007 |
| Stannard, John E. | *Delay in the Performance of Contractual Obligations* [P,A] | | Oxford University Press | 2007 |

## Noteworthy websites, blogs, etc.:

### WEBSITE

- Stewart Dunn, The Law of Damages (http://www.stewartdunn.com/)

# COPYRIGHT

Copyright is a particular subset of intellectual property law which deals with the right to reproduce, publish, broadcast, or perform protected works. This topic is largely rooted in statutory law, primarily portions of the Copyright, Designs and Patents Act 1988 and the Copyright Act 1956, which have in turn been interpreted by a large and instructive body of case law. There are also relevant statutory instruments, European Union directives, and international conventions such as WIPO (World Intellectual Property Organisation).

Major divisions within copyright law include Crown and Parliamentary copyright, the Copyright Tribunal, moral rights (also known as 'paternity rights'), design rights, and database protection.

Many of the titles listed under INTELLECTUAL PROPERTY include commentary on the law of copyright.

*Related topic(s): DESIGNS; INFORMATION TECHNOLOGY LAW; INTELLECTUAL PROPERTY LAW; MEDIA and ENTERTAINMENT LAW; TELECOMMUNICATIONS LAW; TRADE MARKS.*

| Author(s) | Title | Edition | Publisher | Year |
|---|---|---|---|---|
| Merkin, Robert and Black, Jack | *Copyright and Design* [P] | | Sweet & Maxwell | LL |
| Vitoria, Mary, *et al.* | *Laddie, Prescott & Vitoria: Modern Law of Copyright and Designs* [P,A] | 4th | LexisNexis Butterworths | 2011 |
| Cornish, William R., Llewelyn, David, and Aplin, Tanya | *Intellectual Property: Patents, Copyright, Trade Marks, and Allied Rights* [S,P,A] | 8th | Sweet & Maxwell | 2013 |
| Garnett, Kevin, Davies, Gillian and Harbottle, Gwilym | *Copinger and Skone James on Copyright* [P,A] | 17th | Sweet & Maxwell | 2015* |
| Garnett, Kevin and Davies, Gillian | *Moral Rights* [P,A] | 2nd | Sweet & Maxwell | 2010 |
| Torremans, Paul | *Holyoak & Torremans Intellectual Property Law* (specifically Part C: Copyright and Related Issues) [S] | 7th | Oxford University Press | 2013 |

| Author(s) | Title | Edition | Publisher | Year |
|---|---|---|---|---|
| Stokes, Simon | *Digital Copyright: Law and Practice* [P] | 4th | Hart Publishing | 2014 |
| Arnold, Richard | *Performers' Rights* [P,A] | 4th | Sweet & Maxwell | 2008 |
| Bently, Lionel and Sherman, Brad | *Intellectual Property Law* (specifically Part I: Copyright) [S,P] | 4th | Oxford University Press | 2014 |
| Jacob, The Rt. Hon. Sir Robin, Alexander, Daniel, and Fisher, Matthew | *A Guidebook to Intellectual Property: Patents, Trade Marks, Copyright and Designs* [S] | 6th | Sweet & Maxwell | 2013 |

## Noteworthy websites, blogs, etc.:

### BLOGS

- Mark Anderson, IP Draughts (https://ipdraughts.wordpress.com/)
- Fieldfisher (firm), Intellectual Property Blog (http://intellectualpropertyblog.fieldfisher.com/)
- LexisNexis, World of IP and IT (WIPIT) Blog (http://blogs.lexisnexis.co.uk/wipit/)
- Shireen Smith, Azrights News and Media (www.venables.co.uk/blogs.htm)
- Neil J. Wilkof, et al., The IPKat (www.ipkat.com)

# CRIMINAL LAW

Criminal Law as a legal topic usually divides into two distinct streams: substantive criminal law and procedural criminal law. The listing below deals almost exclusively with substantive law, although some titles do touch upon the procedural process.

For titles dealing with the procedural facets of criminal law, see PRACTICE & PROCEDURE (CRIMINAL) and for evidence in criminal law, see EVIDENCE.

Substantive criminal issues include the elements of a crime, i.e., *mens rea* and *actus reus*, and concepts such as causation, criminal negligence, strict liability, omission, and mistake *inter alia*. An associated topic is sentencing which is included hereunder. Fundamental principles of criminal law, such as *mens rea* and *actus reus* emerged through the common law and remain rooted there.

Most criminal law statutes such as the Criminal Justice Act 2003 deal more with procedural matters than substantive law. There is no specific criminal code in Britain so criminal offences are found in specific enactments such as the Drugs Act 2005, Forgery and Counterfeiting Act 1981, Offences Against the Person Act 1861, Sexual Offences Act 2003, and Theft Act 1968, among many others. There are also a number of offences which are based solely in common law such as murder, manslaughter, and assault. Such offences have been shaped and developed exclusively by judicial decision over many centuries.

Some titles deal with the relatively new phenomenon of anti-social behaviour orders (ASBOs) which were introduced by the Anti-Social Behaviour Act 2003. While technically a civil remedy, ASBOs deal with a range of behaviours many of which are akin to minor criminal offences.

English criminal law is complicated and complex and requires investigation into a far flung series of statutory provisions and common law principles.

*Related topic(s): EVIDENCE; HUMAN RIGHTS and CIVIL LIBERTIES, INTERNATIONAL CRIMINAL LAW; MENTAL HEALTH LAW; POLICE and PUBLIC ORDER LAW; PRACTICE & PROCEDURE (CRIMINAL).*

| Author(s) | Title | Edition | Publisher | Year |
|---|---|---|---|---|
| Ormerod, David, ed. | *Blackstone's Criminal Practice 2016* [P] | | Oxford University Press | Annual |
| Richardson, P.J., ed. | *Archbold: Criminal Pleading, Evidence, and Practice 2016* [P] | | Sweet & Maxwell | Annual |

| Author(s) | Title | Edition | Publisher | Year |
|---|---|---|---|---|
| Allen, Michael J. and Cooper, Simon | *Elliott and Wood's Cases and Materials on Criminal Law* [S] | 12th | Sweet & Maxwell | 2016 |
| Ashworth, Andrew | *Law in Context: Sentencing and Criminal Justice* [S] | 6th | Cambridge University Press | 2015 |
| Baker, Dennis | *Glanville Williams: Textbook of Criminal Law* [S,A] | 4th | Sweet & Maxwell | 2015 |
| Ormerod, David and Laird, Karl | *Smith and Hogan Criminal Law* [P,S] | 14th | Oxford University Press | 2015 |
| Card, Richard | *Card, Cross & Jones: Criminal Law* [S,P] | 21st | Oxford University Press | 2014 |
| Elliott, Catherine and Quinn, Frances | *Elliott & Quinn: Criminal Law* [S] | 10th | Pearson Education | 2014 |
| Gibson, Bryan | *Criminal Justice: A Beginner's Guide* [N,S] | | Waterside Press | 2014 |
| Glazebrook, Peter, ed. | *Blackstone's Statutes on Criminal Law 2014-15* [P,S] | | Oxford University Press | 2014 |
| Herring, Jonathan | *Criminal Law: Text, Cases, and Materials* [S] | 6th | Oxford University Press | 2014 |
| Keaton, H.M., *et al.* | *Clarkson and Keating: Criminal Law* [S] | 8th | Sweet & Maxwell | 2014 |
| Pinto, Amanda and Evans, Martin | *Corporate Criminal Liability* [P] | 3rd | Sweet & Maxwell | 2013 |
| Simester, A.P. *et al.* | *Simester and Sullivan's Criminal Law* [S] | 5th | Hart Publishing | 2013 |
| Farbey, Judith, Sharpe, Robert, and Atrill, Simon | *The Law of Habeas Corpus* [A,P] | 3rd | Oxford University Press | 2011 |
| Ashworth, Andrew and Redmayne, Michael | *The Criminal Process* [S] | 4th | Oxford University Press | 2010 |
| Rook, Hon. Judge Peter and Ward, Robert | *Sexual Offences: Law & Practice* [P] | 4th | Sweet & Maxwell | 2010 |
| Collins, Scott and Cattermole, Rebecca | *Anti-Social Behaviour and Disorder: Powers and Remedies* [P] | 2nd | Sweet & Maxwell | 2006 |
| Sikand, Maya | *ASBOS: A Practical Guide to Defending Anti-Social Behaviour Orders* [P] | | Legal Action Group | 2006 |

## Noteworthy websites, blogs, etc.:

### WEBSITES

- Criminal Law & Justice Weekly (http://www.criminallawandjustice.co.uk/)
- Crown Prosecution Service (CPS), Legal Guidance (http://www.cps.gov.uk/legal/)
- LexisNexis, Lexis Web: Crime (http://lexisweb.co.uk/groups/crime/default.aspx)

### BLOG

- Dan Bunting, Lyndon Harris, and Sara Williams, UK Criminal Law Blog (http://ukcriminallawblog.com/category/current-awareness/caselaw-update/)

# CROWN LAW

The term “Crown Law” is employed here to suggest three facets of constitutional law related directly to the British Crown; namely, the constitutional underpinnings of the monarchy, legal proceedings by and against the crown and its immunity therefrom, and issues related to crown property.

Important subtopics include the royal prerogative, crown estates and revenues, and escheat (the reversion of ownership of land to the Crown).

Statutes of note are the Crown Proceedings Act 1947, Crown Estate Act 1961, and Civil List Act 1972.

As the monarch is also the head of the Church of England, see also ECCLESIASTICAL LAW.

*Related topic(s): ADMINISTRATIVE LAW; CONSTITUTIONAL LAW; ECCLESIASTICAL LAW; ENGLISH LEGAL SYSTEM; NEGLIGENCE; NUISANCE; TORT LAW.*

| Author(s) | Title | Edition | Publisher | Year |
|---|---|---|---|---|
| Booth, Cherie Q.C. and Squires, Daniel | *The Negligence Liability of Public Authorities* [P,A] | 2nd | Oxford University Press | 2016 |
| Morrell, John and Foster, His Honour Judge Richard | *Local Authority Liability* [P] | 6th | Jordan Publishing | 2015 |
| Moules, Richard | *Actions against Public Officials: Legitimate Expectations, Misstatements and Misconduct* [P,A] | | Sweet & Maxwell | 2009 |
| Sunkin, Maurice and Payne, Sebastian, eds. | *The Nature of the Crown: A Legal and Political Analysis* [A] | | Oxford University Press | 2000 |
| Bogdanor, Vernon | *The Monarchy and the Constitution* [A] | | Oxford University Press | 1997 |
| Edwards, J. Ll. J. | *The Law Officers of the Crown* [A] | | Sweet & Maxwell | 1964 |
| Bell, Ronald McMillan | *Crown Proceedings: Being a Full Statement of the Law Relating to Actions By and Against the Crown as Affected by the Crown Proceedings Act, 1947* [A] | | Sweet & Maxwell | 1948 |

| | | | | |
|---|---|---|---|---|
| Chitty, Joseph | *A Treatise on the Law of the Prerogatives of the Crown* [A] | | Joseph Butterworth | 1820 |

## DATA PROTECTION

Data protection as a legal matter is a particular component of privacy law that deals specifically with protecting an individual's personal data and ensuring that entities which harvest this information do so in accordance with the prescribed controls and safeguards.

The Data Protection Act 1998 is the core piece of domestic legislation which articulates standards for data protection, establishes the Data Protection Tribunal, and brings British law into accord with EC Council Directive 95/46 (protection of individuals with regard to the processing of personal data and on the free movement of such data).

For titles dealing with law of privacy in a more general context, see PRIVACY LAW and for those dealing with access to government information, see FREEDOM of INFORMATION.

*Related topic(s): FREEDOM of INFORMATION; INFORMATION TECHNOLOGY LAW; INTELLECTUAL PROPERTY LAW; LIBEL and SLANDER; PRIVACY LAW.*

| Author(s) | Title | Edition | Publisher | Year |
|---|---|---|---|---|
| Jay, Rosemary, Boardman, Ruth, and Grant, Hazel | *Encyclopedia of Data Protection and Privacy* [P] | | Sweet & Maxwell | LL |
| Millard, Christopher, ed. | *Cloud Computing Law* [A,P] | 2nd | Oxford University Press | 2016 |
| Coppel, Philip | *Information Rights: Law and Practice* [P,A] | 4th | Hart Publishing | 2014 |
| Lambert, Paul | *A User's Guide to Data Protection* [N,S] | | Bloomsbury Professional | 2013 |
| Bessant, Claire and Tompkins, Phil, eds. | *Information Sharing Handbook* [P] | | The Law Society | 2009 |
| Carey, Peter | *Data Protection: A Practical Guide to UK and EU Law* [P] | 4th | Oxford University Press | 2015 |
| Room, Stewart | *Butterworths Data Security Law and Practice* [P] | | LexisNexis Butterworths | 2009 |
| Jay, Rosemary | *Data Protection: Law and Practice* [P] | 4th | Sweet & Maxwell | 2014 |
| Singleton, Susan | *Tolley's Data Protection Handbook* [P] | 4th | LexisNexis Butterworths | 2006 |

## Noteworthy websites, blogs, etc.:

### BLOGS

- Amberhawk Associates, Hawktalk (http://amberhawk.typepad.com/amberhawk/)
- Fieldfisher (firm), Privacy and Information Law Blog (http://privacylawblog.fieldfisher.com/)
- Information Commissioner's Office, ICO Blog (https://iconewsblog.wordpress.com/)
- Olswang (firm), Datonomy: The Data Protection Blog (http://datonomy.eu/)
- Timothy Pitt-Payne, Anya Proops, Robin Hopkins, and Christopher Knight, Panopticon (http://panopticonblog.com/)
- RPC (firm), RPC Data and Privacy Law (http://www.rpc.co.uk/index.php?option=com_easyblog&view=latest&Itemid=107)
- Tim Turner, 2040 Information Law Blog (http://2040infolawblog.com/)

# DEBTOR & CREDITOR LAW

This topic deals with the rights and obligations of debtors and creditors usually with regard to unpaid debt. It is often subsumed under the topic of Insolvency but not all debtor/creditor relationships arise in the context of insolvency, so rather than dealing with bankruptcy proceedings, the titles listed below deal almost exclusively with the ways in which creditors may recover unpaid debts.

Subtopics include choses-in-action, consumer credit, hire/purchase arrangements, security, and enforcement of debt. Leading statutes are the Consumer Credit Act 1974 and the Consumer Credit Act 2006 for debt related to purchases by consumers and the Tribunals, Courts and Enforcement Act 2007 for debts being enforced under court order.

For debts in the context of a bankruptcy or insolvency, see INSOLVENCY LAW.

*Related topic(s): CONSUMER LAW; CONTRACT LAW; INSOLVENCY LAW; PROPERTY LAW.*

| Author(s) | Title | Edition | Publisher | Year |
|---|---|---|---|---|
| Sandbrook, Claire | *Enforcement of a Judgment* [P] | 12th | Sweet & Maxwell | 2015 |
| Levaggi, Peter, Marsden, David, and Mooney, Peter | *Enforcement and Debt Recovery* [P] | 2nd | The Law Society | 2014 |
| Kruse, John | *Debt Recovery in the Courts* [P] | | Wildy, Simmonds & Hill | 2010 |
| Kruse, John | *The Law of Seizure of Goods: Debtors Rights and Remedies* [P] | 2nd | XPL Law | 2009 |
| Sandbrook, Claire | *Debt Recovery through the Courts* [P] | | Sweet & Maxwell | 2008 |

## Noteworthy websites, blogs, etc.:

### WEBSITE

- Jordan Publishing, Jordan's Insolvency Law: Latest Cases (http://www.jordanpublishing.co.uk/practice-areas/insolvency/news_and_comment?filter[category_id]=2751)

# DESIGNS

This is a specific subset of intellectual property law dealing with the protection of designs (both two dimensional and three dimensional). The law with regard to designs (also known as industrial designs) is complex as designs can be protected by the European Union or by the United Kingdom and in both cases they can be registered or unregistered. As a result, while the protections afforded are largely similar, there are some differences in the manners in which they are attained and the requirements of registration making protection of an industrial design a more complicated matter than one might first imagine.

The protection of an industrial design can be traced originally to copyright law, originally to textile design in the eighteenth century. The Copyright of Designs Act 1839 (2 Vict., cap. 17) was the first statute to specifically prohibit illicit copying of a design by providing protection in its preamble "for the shape or configuration of any article of manufacture. . . ."

Currently the statutory provisions of note are sections of the Registered Designs Act 1949 and to a lesser extent the Copyright, Designs and Patents Act 1988. There are numerous statutory instruments and European directives and regulations.

Basic subtopics of the subject include *inter alia* requirements for protection such as of novelty of design, registration procedure, terms of protection, infringement, and damages.

*Related topic(s): COPYRIGHT, INTELLECTUAL PROPERTY, PATENTS.*

| Author(s) | Title | Edition | Publisher | Year |
|---|---|---|---|---|
| Merkin, Robert and Black, Jack | *Copyright and Designs Law* [P] | | Sweet & Maxwell | LL |
| Flint, Michael, Fitzpatrick, Nicholas, and Thorne, Clive | *A User's Guide to Design Law* [P] | 7th | Bloomsbury Professional | 2016 |
| Jacob, The Rt. Hon. Sir Robin, Alexander, Daniel, and Fisher, Matthew | *A Guidebook to Intellectual Property* [S,N] | | Hart Publishing | 2013 |
| Vitoria, Mary, *et al.* | *Laddie, Prescott & Vitoria: Modern Law of Copyright and Designs* [P,A] | 4th | LexisNexis Butterworths | 2011 |

| | | | | |
|---|---|---|---|---|
| Howe, Martin | *Russell-Clarke and Howe on Industrial Designs* [P,A] | 8th | Sweet & Maxwell | 2010 |
| Sykes, John | *Intellectual Property in Designs* [P,A] | | LexisNexis Butterworths | 2005 |

## Noteworthy websites, blogs, etc.:

### BLOGS

- Mark Anderson, IP Draughts (https://ipdraughts.wordpress.com/)
- Fieldfisher (firm), Intellectual Property Blog (http://intellectualpropertyblog.fieldfisher.com/)
- LexisNexis, World of IP and IT (WIPIT) Blog (http://blogs.lexisnexis.co.uk/wipit/)
- Shireen Smith, Azrights News and Media (www.venables.co.uk/blogs.htm)
- Neil J. Wilkof, et al., The IPKat (www.ipkat.com)

# DISCRIMINATION LAW

The law prohibiting discrimination is rooted almost entirely in domestic legislation, European directives, and international agreements with a profound body of jurisprudence assisting in the interpretation and application of these legislative enactments. There had long been a series of statutes dealing with specific types of discrimination but the Equality Act 2010 has essentially brought all prohibited grounds of discrimination under one umbrella.

Discrimination can be either direct or indirect and the most commonly litigated matters are discrimination with regard to: age, disability, race, religion or belief, sex, and sexual orientation.

It is important to note that the texts listed below which were published prior to 2011 do not reflect all the changes brought about by the Equality Act 2010 and therefore portions of them will be outdated. The newer publications and editions deal with the subject in the context of the new Act.

*Related topic(s): ADMINISTRATIVE LAW; CONSTITUTIONAL LAW; EMPLOYMENT and LABOUR LAW; HUMAN RIGHTS and CIVIL LIBERTIES; MARRIAGE and CIVIL PARTNERSHIPS.*

| Author(s) | Title | Edition | Publisher | Year |
|---|---|---|---|---|
| Hughes, Pauline, ed. | *Discrimination Law* [P] | | Bloomsbury Professional | LL |
| Tucker, Katherine and George, Sarah | *Discrimination in Employment* [P] | | Sweet & Maxwell | LL |
| Rubenstein, Michael | *Discrimination: A Guide to the Relevant Case Law* [P] | 28th | Rubenstein Publishing | 2015 |
| McColgan, Aileen | *Discrimination, Equality and the Law* [A,S] | | Hart Publishing | 2014 |
| Jackson, Karen and Banerjee, Lydia | *Disability Discrimination: Law and Case Management* [P] | | The Law Society | 2013 |
| Monaghan, Karon Q.C. | *Monaghan on Equality Law* [P,A] | 2nd | Oxford University Press | 2013 |
| Connolly, Michael | *Discrimination Law* [S] | 2nd | Sweet & Maxwell | 2011 |
| Gregory, Sarah and Temperton, Ellen | *Tolley's Discrimination in Employment Handbook* [P] | 2nd | LexisNexis Butterworths | 2011 |
| Doyle, Brian J., *et al.* | *Equality and Discrimination: The New Law* [P] | | Jordan Publishing | 2010 |

| Author(s) | Title | Edition | Publisher | Year |
|---|---|---|---|---|
| Duggan, Michael | *Equality Act 2010: A Guide to the New Law* [P] | | The Law Society | 2010 |
| Keen, Spencer and Oulton, Richard | *Disability Discrimination in Employment* [P] | | Oxford University Press | 2009 |
| Doyle, Brian J. | *Disability Discrimination: Law and Practice* [P] | 6th | Jordan Publishing | 2008 |
| Davies, James, ed. | *Age Discrimination* [P,A] | | Bloomsbury Professional | 2007 |
| Addison, Neil | *Religious Discrimination and Hatred Law* [A,S] 🖰 | | Routledge-Cavendish | 2006 |
| Palmer, Camilla, *et al.* | *Discrimination Law Handbook* [P] | 2nd | Legal Action Group | 2006 |

## Noteworthy websites, blogs, etc.:

### BLOGS

- 1 Crown Office Row, UK Human Rights Blog (http://ukhumanrightsblog.com/)
- Antoine Buyse, ed., ECHR (European Convention on Human Rights and Fundamental Freedoms) (http://echrblog.blogspot.co.uk/)
- Legal Action Group, Legal Action Group News & Blog (http://www.legalactiongroupnews.org.uk/)
- Oxford Human Rights Hub, Oxford Human Rights Hub (http://ohrh.law.ox.ac.uk/blog/)

# DRAFTING and LEGAL WRITING

The ability to communicate effectively is a critical skill for the modern legal practitioner. Solicitors are frequently called upon to write various memoranda-of-law, opinion pieces, and court briefs, etc. Moreover they will be asked to draft various contracts and all manner of agreements. Legal writing is a most unique form of writing and employs a radically different set of skills than other styles of writing. There are many works which provide direction and advice to lawyers with regard to this unique art.

*Related topic(s): ADVOCACY; LEGAL SKILLS and METHOD; STATUTORY INTERPRETATION and LEGISLATIVE DRAFTING.*

| Author(s) | Title | Edition | Publisher | Year |
|---|---|---|---|---|
| Webley, Lisa | *Legal Writing* [S] | 4th | Routledge | 2016 |
| Haigh, Rupert | *Legal English* [S] | 4th | Routledge-Cavendish | 2015 |
| Emmet, David | *Bar Manual: Legal Drafting* [S,P] | 17th | Oxford University Press | 2014 |
| Butt, Peter | *Modern Legal Drafting: A Guide to Using Clearer Language* [S] | 3rd | Cambridge University Press | 2013 |
| Rose, William and Eastman, Roger | *Pleadings without Tears: A Guide to Legal Drafting under the Civil Procedure Rules* [S,P] | 8th | Oxford University Press | 2012 |
| McKay, William R. and Charlton, Helen E. | *Legal English: How to Understand and Master the Language of Law* [S] | 2nd | Pearson Education | 2011 |
| Powell, Dave and Teare, Emma | *Writing for Law* [S] | | Palgrave Macmillan | 2010 |
| Zillman, Donald N. and Roth, Evan J. | *Strategic Legal Writing* [S] | | Cambridge University Press (US) | 2008 |
| Adler, Mark | *Clarity for Lawyers: Effective Legal Writing* [P,S] | 2nd | The Law Society | 2006 |

## ECCLESIASTICAL LAW

Normally the term 'ecclesiastical law' refers to the operation of the Church of England and its internal mechanisms for administrating canon law. However, the list below presumes a broader scope and includes both the above and also religious law in general.

The major subtopics within this subject include the constitution of the Church of England, its property, its ecclesiastical jurisdiction (e.g., discipline of clergy), cathedrals, and the status of other denominations.

The primary statutory provisions are synod measures such as the Church of England (Worship and Doctrine) Measure 1974, Ecclesiastical Jurisdiction Measure 1963, Pastoral Measure 1968, Cathedrals Measure 1999, Clergy Discipline Measure 1999, and Synodical Government Measure 1969.

*Related topic(s): CONSTITUTIONAL LAW; CROWN LAW; ENGLISH LEGAL SYSTEM.*

| Author(s) | Title | Edition | Publisher | Year |
|---|---|---|---|---|
| Ferrari, Silvio, ed. | *Routledge Handbook of Law and Religion* [A,S,N] | | Routledge | 2015 |
| Hill, Mark, Sandberg, Russell, and Doe, Norman | *Religion and the Law in the United Kingdom* [A,P,S] | 2nd | Kluwer Law International | 2014 |
| Briden, Timothy, ed. | *Moore's Introduction to English Canon Law* [P,A,N] | 4th | Bloomsbury Continuum | 2013 |
| Rivers, Julian | *The Law of Organized Religions: Between Establishment and Secularism* [A] | | Oxford University Press | 2010 |
| Hill, Mark | *Ecclesiastical Law* [P,A] | 3rd | Oxford University Press | 2007 |
| Legal Advisory Commission of General Synod | *Legal Opinions Concerning the Church of England* [A] | 8th | Church House Publishing | 2007 |
| Derriman, James | *Chancel Repair Liability: How to Research It* [N,P] | | Wildy, Simmonds & Hill | 2006 |
| Doe, Norman | *The Law of the Church in Wales* [P,A] | | U. of Wales Press | 2002 |

| | | | | |
|---|---|---|---|---|
| Dale, Sir William | *The Law of the Parish Church* [P,A] | 7th | LexisNexis Butterworths | 1998 |
| Doe, Norman, Hill, Mark, and Ombres, Robert, eds. | *English Canon Law* [A] | | University of Wales Press | 1998 |
| Bursell, Rupert D.H. | *Liturgy, Order, and the Law* [A] | | Oxford University Press | 1997 |
| Leeder, Lynne | *Ecclesiastical Law Handbook* [P,A] | | Sweet & Maxwell | 1997 |

# EDUCATION LAW

The law of schools and post-secondary education in England is primarily found in a series of statutes with a sizable body of jurisprudence providing interpretation of them and guidance with regard to their application. The most important statute is the Education Act 1996, which subsumed major portions of the Education Act 1944, with regard to nursery, primary, and secondary education and the Further and Higher Education Act 1992 when dealing with post-secondary and sixth form institutions. These statutes deal with both independent and publicly-funded schools. Other important statutes include the Learning and Skills Act 2000, the Academies Act 2010, and the School Standards and Framework Act 1998.

There is also notable European law in this field by way of the Convention for the Protection of Human Rights and Fundamental Freedoms, the first protocol of which provides a right to education.

Relevant case law tends to deal primarily with duties and standards of care expected of teachers and educational institutions.

Important subtopics of Education Law are, *inter alia*, local education authorities, the governance of schools, and curricular matters.

| Author(s) | Title | Edition | Publisher | Year |
|---|---|---|---|---|
| Booth, Cherie, Coleman, John, and Widdrington, Tony | *The Law of Education* [P] | | LexisNexis Butterworths | LL |
| Freckelton, Ian | *Scholarly Misconduct: Law, Regulation and Practice* [A,P,S] | | Oxford University Press | 2016 |
| Ford, John, Hughes, Mary, and May, Karen | *Education Law and Practice* [P] | 3rd | Jordan Publishing | 2010 |
| Farrington, Dennis J. and Palfreyman, David | *The Law of Higher Education* [P] | 2nd | Oxford University Press | 2012 |
| McManus, J. Richard | *Education and the Courts* [P,A] | 3rd | Jordan Publishing | 2012 |
| Jackman, Angela, Hay, Deborah, and Wilkins, Pat | *Practical Education Law* [P] | | The Law Society | 2005 |
| Hyams, Oliver | *Law of Education* [P] | 2nd | Jordan Publishing | 2004 |

## Noteworthy websites, blogs, etc.:

### BLOG

- Marc Beaumont, Barrister, Blog (http://www.marcbeaumont.typepad.com/)

## EMPLOYMENT and LABOUR LAW

Employment and Labour Law is a broad topic which deals with the law of employment in both the trade union (labour) and non-union (employment) environments. Its major subtopics include contracts of employment, employees' rights, discipline and termination, unfair/wrongful dismissal, and industrial relations among others.

This is essentially a legislation-based area of law with major statutes being the Employment Rights Act 1996, the Trade Union and Labour Relations (Consolidation) Act 1992, and the Employment Tribunals Act 1996. There are also numerous relevant statutory instruments and important European Union directives in relation to working conditions. A very instructive quasi-legislative provision is the Code of Practice of the ACAS (Advisory, Conciliation, and Arbitration Service) which is subsumed under the Trade Union and Labour Relations (Consolidation) Act 1992 and spells out the prescribed dismissal, discipline and grievance procedures to be followed by employers.

*Related topic(s): CONTRACT LAW; DISCRIMINATION LAW; HUMAN RIGHTS and CIVIL LIBERTIES.*

| Author(s) | Title | Edition | Publisher | Year |
|---|---|---|---|---|
| | *Sweet & Maxwell's Encyclopedia of Employment Law* [P] | | Sweet & Maxwell | LL |
| Aarons, Elaine | *Termination of Employment* [P] | | Bloomsbury Professional | LL |
| Mahal, Ravinder, ed. | *Tolley's Employment Law Service* [P] | | LexisNexis Butterworths | LL |
| Tucker, Katherine and George, Sarah | *Discrimination in Employment* [P] | | Sweet & Maxwell | LL |
| Mansfield, Gavin, Bowers, John, and Macmillan, John, eds. | *Blackstone's Employment Law Practice 2014* [P] | | Oxford University Press | Annual |
| Slade, Mrs. Justice Elizabeth, *et al.* | *Tolley's Employment Law Handbook* [P] | 29th | LexisNexis Butterworths | Annual |
| Wallington, Peter, Q.C. | *Butterworths Employment Law Handbook* [P] | 23rd | LexisNexis Butterworths | Annual |
| Howard, Gillian | *Drafting Employment Contracts* [P] | 3rd | The Law Society | 2016 |

| Author(s) | Title | Edition | Publisher | Year |
|---|---|---|---|---|
| Duggan, Michael | Contracts of Employment: Law and Guidance [P] | 4th | Duggan Press | 2015 |
| Gould, Tony | *Unfair Dismissal: A Guide to Relevant Case Law* [P] | 33rd | LexisNexis Butterworths | 2015 |
| Keall, Sian, ed. | *Employment and Labour Law* [P] | 6th | Sweet & Maxwell | 2015 |
| Kidner, Richard, ed. | *Blackstone's Statutes on Employment Law 2015-2016* [S,P] | | Oxford University Press | 2015 |
| Smith, Ian and Baker, Aaron | *Smith and Wood's Employment Law* [S,P] | 12th | Oxford University Press | 2015 |
| Astra, Emir | *Selwyn's Law of Employment* [S,P] | 18th | Oxford University Press | 2014 |
| Barnett, Daniel, Gore, Keira, and Scrope, Henry | *Employment Law Handbook* [P] | 6th | The Law Society | 2014 |
| Pitt, Gwyneth | *Employment Law* [S] | 9th | Sweet & Maxwell | 2014 |
| Bennett, Daniel, ed. | *Munkman on Employers' Liability* [P] | 16th | LexisNexis Butterworths | 2013 |
| Deakin, Simon and Morris, Gillian S. | *Labour Law* [S] | 6th | Hart Publishing | 2012 |
| Bowers, John and Davis, Carol | *Termination of Employment* [P] | 5th | Wildy, Simmonds & Hill | 2010 |
| Collins, Hugh | *Employment Law* [S] | 2nd | Oxford University Press | 2010 |

## Noteworthy websites, blogs, etc.:

### WEBSITES

- Bath Publishing, Employment Cases Update (http://www.employmentcasesupdate.co.uk/site.aspx?i=ho0)
- Herbert Smith Freehills, Employment Notes (http://hsfnotes.com/employment/)
- Jordan Publishing, Jordan's Employment Law: Case Summaries (http://www.jordanpublishing.co.uk/practice-areas/employment/news_and_comment?filter[category_id]=2479)
- LexisNexis, Lexis Web: Employment (http://lexisweb.co.uk/groups/employment/default.aspx)

**BLOGS**

- Fieldfisher, Fieldfisher Employment Law Blog (http://employmentlawblog.fieldfisher.com/)
- Philip Henson, Employment Law Update (https://employmentlawupdate.wordpress.com)
- Legal Action Group, Legal Action Group News & Blog (http://www.legalactiongroupnews.org.uk/)
- Belinda Lester, Belinda Lester Talks Employment Law (https://belindalester.wordpress.com/)
- PJH Law, Employment Law Blog (http://www.pjhlaw.co.uk/blog-categories)
- Charles Price, Employment Law Blog (http://employmentlawuk.blogspot.co.uk/)
- Lena Rebane, et al., 12CP Employment Team (http://12cpemploymentteam.blogspot.co.uk)

## ENERGY and NATURAL RESOURCES LAW

This wide and diverse topic includes titles related to gas, electricity, oil, petroleum, coal, and nuclear energy production. The law with regard to the above activities is found almost exclusively in statutes specific to each of them, for example, the Atomic Energy Authority Act 1984, Electricity Act 1986, Gas Act 1986, Coal Industry Act 1994, and Petroleum Act 1998. There are also important statutes of more general application namely the Utilities Act 2000 and Energy Act 2004. There is also a plethora of statutory instruments and European Union directives regulating these undertakings as well as a number of international treaties and conventions.

These industries are closely regulated and monitored by the government with the Secretary of State for Energy and Climate Change being responsible for their oversight. The Secretary may also make direction with regard to energy conservation and initiatives to combat climate change and is empowered by the Climate Change Act 2008 to monitor net carbon use in order to achieve benchmarks established by the Kyoto Protocol of 2005.

An important collateral topic is that of the taxation of energy production.

*Related topic(s): ENVIRONMENTAL LAW; INTERNATIONAL LAW; LOCAL GOVERNMENT LAW; NUISANCE; PLANNING LAW; PROPERTY LAW; TAXATION.*

| **Author(s)** | **Title** | **Edition** | **Publisher** | **Year** |
|---|---|---|---|---|
| Daintith, Terence and Hewitt, Geoff | *United Kingdom Oil and Gas Law* [P] | | Sweet & Maxwell | LL |
| Picton-Turbervill, Geoffrey | *Oil and Gas: A Practical Handbook* [P] | 2nd | Globe Law and Business | 2014 |
| Roberts, Peter | *Gas and LNG Sales and Transportation Agreements: Principles and Practice* [P] | 4th | Sweet & Maxwell | 2014 |
| Alramahi, Moe, Karlberg, John, and Moller, Leon | *Oil and Gas Law in the UK* [P,A,S] | | Bloomsbury Professional | 2013 |
| Griffin, Paul | *Liquefied Natural Gas: The Business of LNG* [P] | 2nd | Globe Law and Business | 2012 |
| Park, Patricia | *Energy Law in the United Kingdom* [P] | | Kluwer Law International | 2012 |
| Gordon, Greg and Paterson, John | *Oil and Gas Law: Current Practice and Emerging Trends* [P] | 2nd | Dundee University Press | 2011 |

| Author(s) | Title | Edition | Publisher | Year |
|---|---|---|---|---|
| Bonass, Matt and Rudd, Michael | Renewables: A Practical Handbook [P] | | Globe Law and Business | 2010 |
| Tromans, Stephen | *Nuclear Law: The Law Applying to Nuclear Installations and Radioactive Substances in Its Historic Context* [P,A] | 2nd | Hart | 2010 |
| Jennings, Anthony | *Oil and Gas Production Contracts* [P] | | Sweet & Maxwell | 2008 |
| Wils, John and Neilson, Ewan C. | *The Technical and Legal Guide to the UK Oil and Gas Industry* [P] | | Abelour Press | 2007 |

# ENGLISH LEGAL SYSTEM

Titles listed hereunder deal with the structural workings of the legal system of England and in some cases, the United Kingdom, and provide understanding of the manner in which legislation and jurisprudence shape the law, and the roles of Parliament, courts, tribunals and commissions, the police and other authorities, the legal profession, and the European Union in creating, interpreting, applying, and enforcing the law.

*Related topic(s): CONSTITUTIONAL LAW; EUROPEAN UNION LAW.*

| Author(s) | Title | Edition | Publisher | Year |
|---|---|---|---|---|
| Slapper, Gary | *How the Law Works* [S,N] | 4th | Routledge | 2016 |
| Elliott, Catherine and Quinn, Frances | *Elliott & Quinn: English Legal System* [S] | 16th | Pearson Education | 2015 |
| Gillespie, Alisdair | *The English Legal System* [S] | 5th | Oxford University Press | 2015 |
| Partington, Martin | *Introduction to the English Legal System 2015-2016* [S] | | Oxford University Press | 2015 |
| Boylan-Kemp, Jo | *English Legal System: The Fundamentals* [S] | 3rd | Sweet & Maxwell | 2014 |
| Darbyshire, Penny | *Darbyshire on the English Legal System* [S] | 11th | Sweet & Maxwell | 2014 |
| Huxley-Binns, Rebecca and Martin, Jacqueline | *Unlocking the English Legal System* [S] | 4th | Hodder Education | 2014 |
| Samuel, Geoffrey | *A Short Introduction to the Common Law* [S,N] | | Edward Elgar | 2014 |
| Burrows, Andrew | *English Private Law* [P] | 3rd | Oxford University Press | 2013 |
| Martin, Jacqueline | *The English Legal System* [S] | 7th | Hodder Education | 2013 |
| Smith, A.T.H. | *Glanville Williams: Learning the Law* [S,N] | 15th | Sweet & Maxwell | 2013 |
| Wild, Charles and Weinstein, Stuart | *Smith & Keenan's English Law* [S] | 17th | Pearson Education | 2013 |
| Rivlin, Geoffrey | *Understanding the Law* [S,N] | 6th | Oxford University Press | 2012 |
| Ward, Richard and Akhtar, Amanda | *Walker & Walker's English Legal System* [S] | 11th | Oxford University Press | 2011 |

| Author(s) | Title | Edition | Publisher | Year |
|---|---|---|---|---|
| Ingman, Terence | *The English Legal Process* [S] | 13th | Oxford University Press | 2010 |
| Zander, Michael | *Law in Context: Cases and Materials on the English Legal System* [S] | 10th | Cambridge University Press | 2007 |

## Noteworthy websites, blogs, etc.:

### DATABASE

- HeinOnline, Selden Society Publications and the History of Early English Law (http://heinonline.org.uml.idm.oclc.org/HOL/MarcXMLData?id=selden &collection=selden)

### BLOG

- Tessa Shepperson, History of Law Blog (http://www.historyoflaw.co.uk/)

# ENVIRONMENTAL LAW

The development of the concept of 'Environmental Law' as a specific area of law is a relatively recent phenomenon. It unites under one heading a range of matters related to damage to and preservation of the nation's land and water resources, the air, and its coasts. Most works on the subject deal with the criminal and civil sanctions which exist in order to protect these natural resources.

There are numerous relevant statutes but the most significant is the Environment Act 1995 which among other things established the Environment Agency. This agency is responsible for the enforcement (but not creation) of environmental law and policy principally as regards pollution prevention, water resources and quality, land quality, fisheries, and waste management, among others. Other statutes of note include the Clean Air Act 1993, Control of Pollution Act 1974, and the Environmental Protection Act 1990.

Other matters dealt with in this topic include drainage, noise, nature conservation, and climate change.

*Related topic(s): AGRICULTURAL LAW; CRIMINAL LAW; ENERGY & NATURAL RESOURCES LAW; LOCAL GOVERNMENT LAW; NUISANCE; PLANNING LAW; and TORT LAW.*

| Author(s) | Title | Edition | Publisher | Year |
|---|---|---|---|---|
| | *Encyclopedia of Environmental Law* [P] | | Sweet & Maxwell | LL |
| Bates, John H. | *Water and Drainage Law* [P] | | Sweet & Maxwell | LL |
| Garner, J.F. | *Garner's Environmental Law* [P] | | LexisNexis Butterworths | LL |
| Fogleman, Valerie, Hellawell, Trevor, and Wiseman, Andrew | *Environmental Law Handbook* [P] | 7th | The Law Society | 2010 |
| Bell, Stuart, McGillivray, Donald, and Pedersen, Ole W. | *Environmental Law* [A,S] | 8th | Oxford University Press | 2013 |
| Wolf, Susan and Stanley, Neil | *Wolf and Stanley on Environmental Law* [S] | 6th | Routledge | 2013 |

| Author(s) | Title | Edition | Publisher | Year |
|---|---|---|---|---|
| Macrory, Richard | *Regulation, Enforcement, and Governance in Environmental Law* [A,P] | 2nd | Hart Publishing | 2014 |
| Reid, Colin T. | *Nature Conservation Law* [P,A] | 3rd | Sweet & Maxwell | 2009 |
| Stookes, Paul | *A Practical Approach to Environmental Law* [P,S] | 2nd | Oxford University Press | 2009 |
| Waite, Andrew, Jones, Gregory, and Fogleman, Valerie | *Environmental Law in Property Transactions* [P] | 4th | Bloomsbury Professional | 2015 |
| Woolley, David, *et al.*, eds. | *Environmental Law* [P] | 2nd | Oxford University Press | 2009 |
| Burnett-Hall, Richard and Jones, Brian | *Burnett-Hall on Environmental Law* [P,A] | 3rd | Sweet & Maxwell | 2012 |
| Bates, John H., Birtles, William, and Pugh, Charles | *Liability for Environmental Harm* [P,A] | | LexisNexis Butterworths | 2004 |

## Noteworthy websites, blogs, etc.:

### WEBSITE

- LexisNexis, Lexis Web: Environment (http://lexisweb.co.uk/groups/environment/default.aspx)

### BLOG

- LexisNexis, Purpose Built Blog (http://blogs.lexisnexis.co.uk/purposebuilt/)

# EQUITY & TRUSTS

Although equity ceased to exist as a distinct entity from the common law with the enactment of the Supreme Court of Judicature Act 1873, it continues as a conceptual framework and a number of its creations, most notably the trust and some specific remedies, remain commonplace today. The Court of Chancery, which was the original court of equity emerged in mediaeval times as an alternative to the sometimes harsh and seemingly unjust rulings of the common law courts which were prone to follow established rules and precedence even at the expense of a fair and just result.

Equity in the modern context usually refers to concepts such as equitable defences, equitable interest in property, and equitable remedies such as injunction, laches, and specific performance, to name but three.

Trusts as a legal topic is frequently paired with equity as it continues to be the most commonly encountered creature of equity in modern law. A trust is essentially a legal arrangement whereby one party, a trustee, exercises control over property for the benefit of another party, a beneficiary (or cestui que trust).

Much of the law of trusts comes to us from the realm of equity but there are a few statutes which speak to the subject: the Trustee Act 2000, Charities Act 2011, and the Trusts of Land and Apportionment of Trustees Act 1996 being three examples.

Texts dealing with trusts usually touch upon subjects such as the various types of trust (express, implied, constructive, e.g.), the requirements of a trust, the powers and duties of trustees, the rights of the beneficiaries, trust administration, and the procedure for varying or terminating a trust.

*Related topic(s): CHARITIES; CONSTITUTIONAL LAW; ENGLISH LEGAL SYSTEM; PROPERTY LAW; REAL PROPERTY; WILLS and PROBATE.*

| Author(s) | Title | Edition | Publisher | Year |
|---|---|---|---|---|
| Clutton, Owen and Jennings, Simon | *Tolley's Administration of Trusts* [P] | | LexisNexis Butterworths | LL |
| Hayton, David, Matthews, Paul, and Mitchell, Charles | *Underhill and Layton: Law of Trusts and Trustees* [P,A] | 19th | LexisNexis Butterworths | 2016 |
| Hudson, Alastair | *Text, Cases and Materials on Equity and Trusts* [S] | | Routledge | 2016 |

| Author(s) | Title | Edition | Publisher | Year |
|---|---|---|---|---|
| Glister, Jamie and Lee, James | Hanbury and Martin: Modern Equity [S,P,A] | 20th | Sweet & Maxwell | 2015 |
| McFarlane, Ben and Mitchell, Charles | *Hayton & Mitchell: Text, Cases and Materials on the Law of Trusts and Equitable Remedies* [S] | 14th | Sweet & Maxwell | 2015 |
| McGhee, John, ed. | *Snell's Equity* [P] | 33rd | Sweet & Maxwell | 2015* |
| Haley, Michael and McMurtry, Lara | *Equity & Trusts* [S] | 4th | Sweet & Maxwell | 2014 |
| Pearce, Robert and Barr, Warren | *Pearce & Stevens' Trusts and Equitable Obligations* [S] | 6th | Oxford University Press | 2014 |
| Penner, J. E. | *The Law of Trusts* [S] | 9th | Oxford University Press | 2014 |
| Watt, Gary | *Trusts and Equity* [S] | 6th | Oxford University Press | 2014 |
| Thurston, John | *A Practitioner's Guide to Trusts* [P] | 10th | Bloomsbury Professional | 2013 |
| Kessler, James and Sartin, Leon | *Drafting Trusts and Will Trusts: A Modern Approach* [P] | 11th | Sweet & Maxwell | 2012 |
| Pettit, Philip H. | *Equity and the Law of Trusts* [S,A] | 12th | Oxford University Press | 2012 |
| Mitchell, Charles | *Constructive and Resulting Trusts* [A] | | Hart Publishing | 2010 |
| Thomas, Geraint and Hudson, Alastair | *The Law of Trusts* [P,A] | 2nd | Oxford University Press | 2010 |
| Burn, E.H. and Virgo, G.I. | *Maudsley & Burns's Trusts & Trustees: Cases and Materials* [S] | 7th | Oxford University Press | 2008 |
| Oakley, A.J. | *Parker and Mellows: The Modern Law of Trusts* [S] | 9th | Sweet & Maxwell | 2008 |
| Mowbray, John, *et al.*, eds. | *Lewin on Trusts* [P,A] | 18th | Sweet & Maxwell | 2007* |
| Worthington, Sarah | *Equity* [S] | 2nd | Oxford University Press | 2006 |

## Noteworthy websites, blogs, etc.:

### BLOG

- Society of Trust and Estate Practitioners, The STEP Blog (http://blog.step.org/about-2/)

# EUROPEAN UNION LAW

With its admission in 1973 into the European Community, the United Kingdom entered into an entirely new legal regime wherein its law was secondary to that of the European Community. As such, European Union law is not 'foreign' law but is, for the most part, the law of the land in England. Although essentially a creature of international agreement, the European Union is one of much more robust legal effect than is the norm for international entities. Three levels of legal enactment apply in member states: regulations, which apply in full in all member states and require no authorising national legislation; directives, which are addressed to all member states and mandate member states to meet a particular objective by a specified date; and decisions, which have specific application only to whom they have been addressed.

Research into European Union law usually looks into matters such as the legal structure and institutions of the European Union, its enactments and decisions, external relations of the Union, and economic and monetary policy. There are legal subject areas in which the European Union is very active and therefore English legal researchers need include European Union law in their investigation. Examples of areas of law with a sizable overlay of European Union law include agriculture and fisheries, business, competition, environmental protection, human rights, intellectual property, trade, free movement within Europe, and workplace health and safety among many others.

On June 23, 2016 the citizens of the United Kingdom narrowly voted in a national referendum to leave the European Union. The mechanism through which this can be achieved is Article 50 of the Treaty of Lisbon (which is itself a major amendment to the two foundational treaties, Maastricht and Rome). Going forward much of the research and treatment of the European Union in British legal writing will almost certainly deal with the particular rules and procedures of Article 50 and the means by which the United Kingdom can lawfully and satisfactorily extricate itself from the European Union. At the time of this writing, predictions are that this will be achieved sometime between 2018 and 2020.

*Related topic(s): INTERNATIONAL LAW; INTERNATIONAL TRADE LAW.*

| Author(s) | Title | Edition | Publisher | Year |
|---|---|---|---|---|
| Klip, André | *European Criminal Law* [S,A] | 3rd | Intersentia | 2016 |

| Author(s) | Title | Edition | Publisher | Year |
|---|---|---|---|---|
| Barnard, Catherine, ed. | European Union Law [S,A] | | Oxford University Press | 2014 |
| Chalmers, Damian, Davies, Gareth, and Monti, Giorgio | *European Union Law* [S,A] | 3rd | Cambridge University Press | 2014 |
| Hartley, Trevor | *The Foundations of European Union Law* [S] | 8th | Oxford University Press | 2014 |
| Lenaerts, Koen | *EU Procedural Law* [A,P] | | Oxford University Press | 2014 |
| Barnard, Catherine | *The Substantive Law of the EU: The Four Freedoms* [S,A] | 4th | Oxford University Press | 2013 |
| Mathijsen, Pierre | *Mathijsen's Guide to European Law* [S,P] | 11th | Sweet & Maxwell | 2013 |
| Rosas, Allan and Armati, Lorna | *EU Constitutional Law: An Introduction* [S,A] | 2nd | Hart Publishing | 2012 |
| Steiner, Josephine and Woods, Lorna | *EU Law* [S] | 11th | Oxford University Press | 2012 |
| Lenaerts, Koen and Van Nuffel, Piet | *European Union Law* [P,S,A] | 3rd | Sweet & Maxwell | 2011 |
| von Bogdandy, Armin and Bast, Jürgen | *Principles of European Constitutional Law* [S,A] | 2nd | Hart Publishing | 2011 |

## Noteworthy websites, blogs, etc.:

### BLOGS

- Antoine Buyse, ed., ECHR (European Convention on Human Rights and Fundamental Freedoms) (http://echrblog.blogspot.co.uk/)
- Matrix Chambers, EUtopia Law (http://eutopialaw.com/)
- Steve Peers, EU Law Analysis (http://eulawanalysis.blogspot.co.uk/)

# EVIDENCE

Simply put, 'evidence' is that which is put before a court in order to prove or disprove a specific fact. The law of evidence is a fairly complex subject in which a series of rules has evolved over a long period of time. The topic tends to divide into two streams: civil evidence and criminal evidence.

Until the passage of the Civil Procedure Rules of 1998, separate sets of rules of evidence existed for different courts. However, since the passage of the rules of 1998, one set applies in most civil matters in all levels of court from County Court to the Court of Appeal (Civil Division). There are, however, topics to which the rules do not entirely apply, primarily family law, probate, and insolvency, for example.

The rules of criminal evidence were similar to those of the civil side until the 1960s when the enactment of the Criminal Evidence Act 1965 and Criminal Evidence Act 1968 saw the beginnings of a divergence between the two streams which became more pronounced when the Police and Criminal Evidence Act 1984 took effect.

Major statutes and rules of note on the civil side include the Civil Evidence Act 1968, Civil Evidence Act 1972, and Civil Evidence Act 1995 and most importantly the Civil Procedure Rules 1998. With regard to criminal evidence the various Criminal Justice Acts, especially those of 1993 and 2003, the Criminal Procedure and Investigations Act 1996, and the Police and Criminal Evidence Act 1984 are particularly instructive.

A noteworthy recent development is with the regard to the expansion of closed material procedures (which are defined by Part 2 of the Justice and Security Act 2013) wherein evidence (both civil and criminal) is deemed too sensitive for disclosure to anyone other than the trier of the case.

Significant subtopics dealt with in the law of evidence include admissibility, standards of proof, weight, relevance of facts, opinion/expert evidence, documentary evidence, and the testimony of witnesses. Evidence from confessions and admissions is a subtopic of note predominantly in the criminal evidence sphere.

*Related topic(s): CRIMINAL LAW; POLICE and PUBLIC ORDER LAW; PRACTICE & PROCEDURE (CIVIL); PRACTICE & PROCEDURE (CRIMINAL).*

| **Author(s)** | **Title** | **Edition** | **Publisher** | **Year** |
|---|---|---|---|---|
| Richardson, P.J., ed. | *Archbold: Criminal Pleading, Evidence, and Practice 2016* [P] | | Sweet & Maxwell | Annual |

| Author(s) | Title | Edition | Publisher | Year |
|---|---|---|---|---|
| Hollander, Charles | *Documentary Evidence* [P] | 12th | Sweet & Maxwell | 2015 |
| Malek, Hodge M., Auburn, Jonathan, and Bagshaw, Roderick | *Phipson on Evidence* [P,A] | 18th | Sweet & Maxwell | 2015 |
| May, Richard and Powles, Steven | *May on Criminal Evidence* [P] | 6th | Sweet & Maxwell | 2015 |
| Monaghan, Nicola | *Law of Evidence* [S,A] | | Cambridge University Press | 2015 |
| Murphy, Peter | *Murphy on Evidence* [S,P] | 14th | Oxford University Press | 2015 |
| Hodgkinson, Tristam and James, Mark | *Expert Evidence: Law & Practice* [P] | 4th | Sweet & Maxwell | 2014 |
| Keane, Adrian and McKeown, Paul | *The Modern Law of Evidence* [S] | 10th | Oxford University Press | 2014 |
| Passmore, Colin | *Privilege* [P,A,S] | | Sweet & Maxwell | 2013 |
| Mason, Stephen, ed. | *Electronic Evidence* [P] | 3rd | LexisNexis Butterworths | 2012 |
| Roberts, Paul and Zuckerman, Adrian | *Criminal Evidence* [S,P] | 2nd | Oxford University Press | 2010 |
| Tapper, Colin | *Cross & Tapper on Evidence* [P,S] | 12th | Oxford University Press | 2010 |
| Iller, Martin | *Civil Evidence: The Essential Guide* [P] | | Sweet & Maxwell | 2006 |

## Noteworthy websites, blogs, etc.:

### WEBSITES

- The Home Office, Publications re PACE [Police & Criminal Evidence Act] (https://www.gov.uk/government/publications)

# FAMILY LAW

This vast subject normally deals with all matters from commencement of marriage to its dissolution and everything in between including marital property, the care, guardianship, and custody of children, their support and maintenance, and protections from domestic violence. This list, though, deals with all of the above with the exception of marriage and divorce which are covered in MARRIAGE and CIVIL PARTNERSHIPS. Many of the family law texts listed here deal with marriage and divorce but have been chosen for inclusion here for their general and broad approaches to family law.

The principal non-marriage/divorce subtopics are family property, children and responsibilities of parents, guardianship, financial support of children and other family matters, and protection from domestic violence.

This is an area of frequent litigation and therefore there is a huge body of instructive case law, but there are a few core statutes to note, including: the Family Law Act 1986, Matrimonial Causes Act 1973, Children Act 1989, Child Support Act 1991, Protection from Harassment Act 1997, Domestic Violence, Crime and Victims Act 2004. There are also three foundational statutes which, while more relevant to Marriage and Civil Partnerships, do frequently touch upon matters discussed above. They are the Marriage Act 1949, the Civil Partnership Act 2004, and the Marriage (Same Sex Couples) Act 2013.

*Related topic(s): CHILDREN; MARRIAGE and CIVIL PARTNERSHIP; PROPERTY LAW; TAXATION; WILLS and PROBATE.*

| Author(s) | Title | Edition | Publisher | Year |
|---|---|---|---|---|
| Craig, Jane, ed. | *Cohabitation: Law and Precedents* [P] | | Sweet & Maxwell | LL |
| Duckworth, Peter | *Matrimonial Property and Finance* [P] | 6th | Jordan Publishing | LL |
| Howell, Grant and Montgomery, Jonathan, eds. | *Butterworths Family Law Service* [P] 🖱 | | LexisNexis Butterworths | LL |
| Wildblood, Stephen and Eaton, Deborah | *Financial Provision in Family Matters* [P] | | Sweet & Maxwell | LL |

| Author(s) | Title | Edition | Publisher | Year |
|---|---|---|---|---|
| Duffield, Nancy, Kempton, Jacque-line, and Sabine, Christa | *CLP Legal Practice Guides: Family Law and Practice 2016* [P] | | College of Law Publishing | Annual |
| Oldham, Mika, ed. | *Blackstone's Statutes on Family Law 2015-16* [S,P] | | Oxford University Press | Annual |
| Lord Wilson of Culworth, the Rt Hon., Cleary, His Honour Judge Anthony, and Black, the Rt. Hon. Lady Justice, eds. | *Family Court Practice 2015* [P] | | Family Law | Annual |
| Black, Jill, *et al.* | *A Practical Approach to Family Law* [S,P] | 10th | Oxford University Press | 2015 |
| Herring, Jonathan | *Family Law* [S] | 7th | Pearson Education | 2015 |
| Lowe, Nigel and Douglas, Gillian | *Bromley's Family Law* [S,P,A] | 11th | Oxford University Press | 2015 |
| Probert, Rebecca | *Cretney and Probert's Family Law* [S] | 9th | Sweet & Maxwell | 2015 |
| Sheridan, Dennis | *Family Law Arbitration* [P] | | The Law Society | 2014 |
| Standley, Kate | *Palgrave Law Masters: Family Law* [S] | 8th | Palgrave Macmillan | 2013 |
| Masson, Judith, Bailey-Harris, Rebecca, and Probert, Rebecca | *Cretney: Principles of Family Law* [S,P,A] | 8th | Sweet & Maxwell | 2008 |

## Noteworthy websites, blogs, etc.:

### WEBSITES

- Family Law Week, Family Law Week: Judgments (http://www.familylawweek.co.uk/site.aspx?i=fo6)
- Family Law Week, Family Law Week: Legislation (http://www.familylawweek.co.uk/site.aspx?i=fo7)
- Jacqui Gilliatt, Barrister, Four Brick Court: (http://4bc.co.uk/our-people/barristers/jacqui-gilliatt-2/)
- Jordan Publishing, Family Law: Judgments (http://www.familylaw.co.uk/news_and_comment?filter[category_id]=2349)
- Jordan Publishing, Family Law: Legislation and Guidance (http://www.familylaw.co.uk/news_and_comment?filter[category_id]=2355)

**BLOGS**

- Diane Benussi, Family Law Blog (http://www.benussilaw.co.uk/category/family-law-blog/)
- Chris McWatters and Rebekah Wilson (Garden Court Chambers), The World of Family Law (https://gcfamily.wordpress.com/)
- Jo Spain, Family Law Matters (http://www.spainwilliams.com/family/)

## FRANCHISING LAW

The retailing and service sectors of British commerce have become dominated by chain stores and branch outlets in a wide variety of activities across the entire spectrum of commercial activity. These titles deal with the legal particulars of franchising. It is a surprisingly complex area of law in that it touches on many others including commercial law, competition law, contract law, and intellectual property law (i.e., trade marks and in some cases access to patented recipes and formulas).

Subtopics dealt with in this subject include the rights and obligations of franchisors (the parent company) and franchisees (the individual outlet operators) and the franchise contract, trade names and descriptions, passing off, taxation, and unfair trading. Statutes of note include the Business Names Act 1985, Competition Act 1998, Copyright, Designs, and Patents Act 1988, Trade Descriptions Act 1968, and the Trade Marks Act 1994. There are also relevant statutory instruments such as the Trade Mark Rules 1994.

This topic is not to be confused with the common law meaning of 'franchise' which essentially refers to a particular Crown prerogative. For titles related to 'franchise' in this context, see CROWN LAW.

*Related topic(s): AGENCY; COMMERCIAL LAW; COMPANY LAW; COMPETITION LAW; CONSUMER LAW; COPYRIGHT; DESIGNS; INTELLECTUAL PROPERTY LAW; INTERNATIONAL TRADE LAW; PATENTS; SALE of GOODS; TAXATION; TRADE MARKS.*

| Author(s) | Title | Edition | Publisher | Year |
|---|---|---|---|---|
| Pratt, John | *Franchising Law & Practice* [P] | | Sweet & Maxwell | LL |
| Abell, Mark | *The Law and Regulation of Franchising in the EU* [P] | | Edward Elgar | 2013 |
| Hero, Marco | *International Franchising: A Practitioner's Guide* [P] | | Globe Law & Business | 2010 |
| Adams, John N., Hickey, Julian, Prichard Jones, K.V. | *Franchising: Practice and Precedents in Business Format Franchising* [P] | 5th | Tottel | 2005 |
| Mendelsohn, Martin | *Franchising Law* [P] | 2nd | Richmond Law & Tax | 2004 |
| Mendelsohn, Martin | *Negotiating an International Master Franchise Agreement* [P] | | Sweet & Maxwell | 2002 |

# FRAUD and MISREPRESENTATION

Most frequently this topic arises in the context of contract law (and also in tort law). The titles below are somewhat more expansive in that some also deal with criminal fraud. The non-criminal aspects of this topic are rooted almost entirely in the common law with centuries of jurisprudence giving it shape and definition. Subjects of frequent investigation include the actionability of a fraudulent act, the categories of misrepresentation (express, implied, fraudulent, and innocent), damages, rescission of contract, and matters related to third party relief.

Criminal fraud is dealt with extensively in the Theft Act 1978.

*Related topics: COMMERCIAL LAW; CONSUMER LAW; CONTRACT LAW; CRIMINAL LAW; TORT LAW.*

| Author(s) | Title | Edition | Publisher | Year |
|---|---|---|---|---|
| Dobbs, the Honourable Mrs. Justice Linda, Owen, Gerralt, and Summers, Gary, eds. | *Fraud: Law, Practice and Procedure* [P] | | LexisNexis Butterworths | LL |
| Montgomery, Clare and Ormerod, David | *Fraud: Criminal Law and Procedure* [P] | | Oxford University Press | LL |
| Eissa, Adrian, Wells, Colin, and Nathaniel, Rudolph | *Fraud: A Practitioner's Handbook* [P] | | Bloomsbury Professional | 2014 |
| Handley, The Hon. Mr. Justice K.R. | *Spencer Bower & Handley Actionable Misrepresentation* [P] | | LexisNexis Butterworths | 2014 |
| McGrath, Paul, Q.C. | *Commercial Fraud in Civil Practice* [P] | 2nd | Oxford University Press | 2014 |
| Arlidge, Anthony, Milne, Alexander, and Sprenger, Polly | *Arlidge and Parry on Fraud* [P,A] | 4th | Sweet & Maxwell | 2013* |
| Cartwright, John | *Misrepresentation, Mistake, and Non-disclosure* [P,A] | 3rd | Sweet & Maxwell | 2012 |

| Author(s) | Title | Edition | Publisher | Year |
|---|---|---|---|---|
| Farrell, Simon, Q.C., Ladenburg, Guy, and Yeo, Nicholas | *Blackstone's Guide to the Fraud Act 2006* [P,A] | | Oxford University Press | 2007 |
| Ulph, Janet | *Commercial Fraud: Civil Liability for Fraud, Human Rights, and Money Laundering* [P,A] | | Oxford University Press | 2006 |

## Noteworthy websites, blogs, etc.:

### WEBSITE

- Fraud Advisory Panel, Resources (https://www.fraudadvisorypanel.org/resource/)

# FREEDOM of INFORMATION

The term 'freedom of information' when employed as a legal subject has come to mean the right of access of individual citizens to the records of a public authority. It is not, therefore, a privacy or confidence matter (see PRIVACY LAW) but more an administrative matter.

Once governed by a mosaic of legislative provisions and some common law rights of information access, this topic is now governed almost exclusively by two statutes: the Freedom of Information Act 2000 and the Data Protection Act 1998. Sub-topics include the request for information procedure, requirements for compliance, fees, exempt information, enforcement, and the role of the Information Commissioner, a position created pursuant to both the Data Protection Act 1998 and Freedom of Information Act 2000.

*Related topic(s): ADMINISTRATIVE LAW; CROWN LAW; DATA PROTECTION; LOCAL GOVERNMENT LAW; MEDICAL LAW; PLANNING LAW; PRIVACY LAW.*

| Author(s) | Title | Edition | Publisher | Year |
|---|---|---|---|---|
| Macdonald, John, Q.C. and Crail, Ross | *The Law of Freedom of Information* [P,A] | 3rd | Oxford University Press | 2016 |
| Coppel, Philip | *Information Rights: Law and Practice* [P] | 4th | Hart Publishing | 2014 |
| Wadham, John, Harris, Kelly, and Metcalfe, Eric | *Blackstone's Guide to the Freedom of Information Act 2000* [P,S] | 5th | Oxford University Press | 2015 |
| Birkinshaw, Patrick | *Freedom of Information: The Law, the Practice, and the Ideal* [S] | 4th | Cambridge University Press | 2010 |
| Birkinshaw, Patrick | *Government and Information: The Law Relating to Access, Disclosure and their Regulation* [P] | 4th | Bloomsbury Professional | 2010 |
| Carey, Peter and Turle, Marcus, eds. | *Freedom of Information Handbook* [P] | 2nd | The Law Society | 2008 |
| Turle, Marcus | *Freedom of Information Manual* [P] | | Sweet & Maxwell | 2006 |

## Noteworthy websites, blogs, etc.:

### BLOGS

- Timothy Pitt-Payne, Anya Proops, Robin Hopkins, and Christopher Knight, Panopticon (http://panopticonblog.com/)

# GAMING and LOTTERIES

Works on this topic deal with all types of gambling including horserace betting, gaming machines, bingos, charity lotteries, and the National Lottery. There was a substantial change to all gambling activities by passage of the Gambling Act 2005 which established a Gambling Commission with power to regulate all facets of gaming in the United Kingdom. It also brought a layer of licensing theretofore unseen by requiring all gaming operations to procure an operating licence from the Gambling Commission and thus providing the commission with an important regulatory tool. There is also a level of local licensing at play too in that a gambling operation with a physical presence, such as a betting shop, must also have a premises licence from their local authority.

Lotteries other than the National Lottery are governed by the Gambling Act 2005 whereas the National Lottery Act 1998 is the principal piece of legislation overseeing the operation of the United Kingdom's large national lottery scheme. This Act established a National Lottery Commission which licences the private sector operators of the National Lottery scheme. The National Lottery Act 1998 also provides guidance and rules with regard to how lottery revenues are to be shared among suitable recipients.

*Related topic(s): ADMINISTRATIVE LAW; CHARITIES; LICENSING LAW; LOCAL GOVERNMENT LAW.*

| Author(s) | Title | Edition | Publisher | Year |
|---|---|---|---|---|
| Phillips, Jeremy, *et al.*, eds. | *Paterson's Licensing Acts 2016* (specifically volume 2: Betting, Gaming and Lotteries) [P] 🖱 | | LexisNexis Butterworths | Annual |
| Phillips, Jeremy, Gouriet, Gerald and Monkcom, Stephen, eds. | *The Law of Gambling* [P] | 4th | Bloomsbury Professional | 2016 |
| Kolvin, Philip, Q.C. | *Gambling for Local Authorities: Licensing, Planning and Regeneration* [P] | 2nd | Institute of Licensing | 2010 |
| Butterfield, Roger | *Gambling and Gaming Licensing: A Practical Guide* [P] | | Shaw & Sons | 2008 |

| Author(s) | Title | Edition | Publisher | Year |
|---|---|---|---|---|
| Rohsler, Carl | Gambling Act 2005—A Current Law Statute Guide [P] | | Sweet & Maxwell | 2005 |

# HEALTH and SAFETY

This topic deals exclusively with the safety and health of workers in the course of their employment and is not a generalised list related to the two topics in other contexts.

The law with regard to workplace health and safety is very much grounded in legislation, the principal statute being the Health and Safety at Work etc. Act 1974. Other statutes of note include the Factories Act 1961 and the Corporate Manslaughter and Corporate Homicide Act 2007. Some statutes deal with health and safety in the context of specific industries, for example the Mines and Quarries Act 1954. There are legion regulations and a number of European Union directives including EC Council Directive 89/391 (on the introduction of measures to encourage improvements in the safety and health of workers at work—as amended) which is known as the "framework" directive and articulates general principles re: worker safety within the European Union.

*Related topic(s): EMPLOYMENT and LABOUR LAW; NEGLIGENCE; TORT LAW.*

| Author(s) | Title | Edition | Publisher | Year |
|---|---|---|---|---|
| Goodman, Michael J., ed. | *Encyclopedia of Health and Safety at Work* [P] | | CCH Editions | LL |
| Bamber, Lawrence, *et al.*, eds. | *Tolley's Health and Safety Handbook 2016* [P] | | LexisNexis Butterworths | Annual |
| Matthews, Richard and Ageros, James | *Health and Safety Enforcement: Law and Practice* [P] | 4th | Oxford University Press | 2016 |
| Moore, Rachel | *The Law of Health and Safety at Work 2015/16* [P] | | Croner | 2015* |
| Clarke, Jonathan, *et al.* | *Redgrave's Health and Safety* [P] | 8th | LexisNexis Butterworths | 2014* |
| Forlin, Gerald and Smail, Louise | *Corporate Liability: Work Related Deaths and Criminal Prosecutions* [P] | 3rd | Bloomsbury Professional | 2014 |
| Channing, John | *Safety at Work* [P] | 8th | Routledge | 2013 |
| Cotter, Barry and Bennett, Daniel, eds. | *Munkman on Employer's Liability* [P] | 15th | LexisNexis Butterworths | 2009 |

## Noteworthy websites, blogs, etc.:

### WEBSITE

- Health and Safety Executive (http://www.hse.gov.uk/)

# HOUSING LAW

These titles deal primarily with housing as a social benefit rather than as a subset of property or construction law. Important matters in this topic include the occupation of housing, whether private or public through housing authorities, homelessness and assistance to the homeless, and the allocation of social housing. Many titles also touch on disrepair and the right to repair.

Legislation to note includes the various iterations of the Housing Act (1985, 1988, 1996, and 2004), the Rent Act 1977, the Local Government and Housing Act 1987, and the Housing and Regeneration Act 2008 under which the Homes and Communities Agency, a function of which is the regulation of social housing, was brought into being.

For titles related to tenants' rights and responsibilities, see RESIDENTIAL TENANCIES LAW. For titles related to building standards, see CONSTRUCTION LAW.

*Related topic(s): CONSTRUCTION LAW; LANDLORD and TENANT LAW; LOANS and MORTGAGES; LOCAL GOVERNMENT LAW; REAL PROPERTY; RESIDENTIAL TENANCIES LAW; SOCIAL SECURITY and WELFARE LAW.*

| Author(s) | Title | Edition | Publisher | Year |
|---|---|---|---|---|
| Arden, Andrew, Q.C., Shepherd, Jim, and Conlan, Tina | *Encyclopedia of Housing Law and Practice* [P] | | Sweet & Maxwell | LL |
| Arden, Andrew and Partington, Martin | *Housing Law* [P] | | Sweet & Maxwell | LL |
| Poynter, Richard and George, Carolyn, *et al.* | *CPAG's Housing Benefit and Council Tax Reduction Legislation 2015/2016* [P] | | Child Poverty Action Group | Annual |
| Astin, Diane | *Housing Law: An Adviser's Handbook* [P] | 3rd | Legal Action Group | 2015 |
| Luba, Jan, Q.C., *et al.* | *Defending Possession Proceedings* [P] | 8th | Legal Action Group | 2015 |
| Luba, Jan, Q.C., Davies, Liz, and Johnston, Connor | *Housing Allocations and Homelessness: Law and Practice* [P] | 4th | Jordan Publishing | 2015 |
| Lister, Sam and Ward, Martin | *Guide to Housing Benefit 2014-17* [P,N] | | Chartered Institute of Housing | 2014* |

| Author(s) | Title | Edition | Publisher | Year |
|---|---|---|---|---|
| Madge, Nic and Madge-Wyld, Sam | *Housing Law Casebook* [P] | 6th | Legal Action Group | 2014 |
| Price, Gail | *Housing Law and Practice 2015* [S,P] | | College of Law Publishing | 2014 |
| Cottle, Stephen, *et al.* | *Housing Law Handbook: A Practical Guide* [P] | | The Law Society | 2009 |
| Carr, Helen, Cottle, Stephen, and Ormandy, David | *Using the Housing Act 2004* [P] | | Jordan Publishing | 2008 |
| Arden, Andrew, Q.C. and Dymond, Andrew | *Manual of Housing Law* [P] | 9th | Sweet & Maxwell | 2012 |

## Noteworthy websites, blogs, etc.:

### BLOGS

- Tessa Shepperson, The Landlord Law Blog (http://www.landlordlawblog.co.uk/)
- The Landlord Law BLOG Case Reports (http://www.landlordlawblog.co.uk/category/law-case-report/)

## HUMAN RIGHTS and CIVIL LIBERTIES

Prior to the coming-into-force in 2000 of the Human Rights Act 1998 (which gave effect to the articles of the European Convention of Human Rights in the United Kingdom) the rights and liberties enjoyed by the English were not articulated in a specific written charter of rights but rather were found in a series of statutes, some of which were longstanding such as the Bills of Rights of 1688 and 1689 and the Habeas Corpus Acts of the seventeenth century, and in a long thread of jurisprudence. In these disparate sources could be found the following rights and protections: freedom of expression, conscience, and religion, of assembly, movement, and association, and the right to life, personal liberty, property, protection under the law, and freedom from arbitrary entry, search or seizure. However, none of the articles providing these protections placed any limits on Parliament or proscribed enactments contrary to the established norms for civil liberties. The European Convention on Human Rights safeguards a number of rights and liberties similar to those protected under English law. Enactments of Parliament must now adhere to the Convention and can be rendered nugatory if they fail to do so. However one of the effects of the Human Rights Act 1998 is to incorporate the rights contained in the European Convention into British statutory law and enables a party to enforce a European Convention right in a British court rather than the European Court of Human Rights in Strasbourg.

The Equality Act 2006 established the Equality and Human Rights Commission. This body came into being in 2007 and has a wide mandate to promote equality and to enforce non-discrimination laws. It has supplanted three former public bodies: the Commission for Racial Equality, the Equal Opportunities Commission, and the Disability Rights Commission.

Specific protections include those related to life and liberty, application of the law, privacy, freedom of conscience, expression, the right to property, freedom of assembly and association, and education and voting rights *inter alia.*

*Related topic(s): CONSTITUTIONAL LAW; CROWN LAW; DISCRIMINATION LAW; EUROPEAN UNION LAW; RESIDENTIAL TENANCIES LAW.*

| Author(s) | Title | Edition | Publisher | Year |
|---|---|---|---|---|
| Simor, Jessica | *Human Rights Practice* [P] | | Sweet & Maxwell | LL |
| McBride, Jeremy, ed. | *Butterworths Human Rights Cases Service 2015* [P] | | LexisNexis Butterworths | Annual |

| Author(s) | Title | Edition | Publisher | Year |
|---|---|---|---|---|
| Fenwick, Helen, Phillipson, Gavin, and Williams, Alexander | Text, Cases and Materials on Public Law and Human Rights [S,A] | 4th | Routledge | 2016 |
| Reid, Karen | *A Practitioner's Guide to the European Convention on Human Rights* [P,A] | 5th | Sweet & Maxwell | 2015 |
| Wadham, John, *et al.* | *Blackstone's Guide to the Human Rights Act 1998* [P] | 7th | Oxford University Press | 2015 |
| Rainey, Bernadette, Wicks, Elizabeth, and Ovey, Clare | *Jacobs, White, & Ovey: The European Convention on Human Rights* [S] | 6th | Oxford University Press | 2014 |
| Davis, Howard | *Human Rights Law Directions* [S] | 3rd | Oxford University Press | 2013 |
| Hoffman, David and Rowe, John | *Human Rights in the UK: An Introduction to the Human Rights Act 1998* [S] | 4th | Pearson Education | 2013 |
| Emmerson, Ben, Ashworth, Andrew, and MacDonald, Alison, eds. | *Human Rights and Criminal Justice* [A,P,S] | 3rd | Sweet & Maxwell | 2012 |
| Clayton, Richard and Tomlinson, Hugh | *The Law of Human Rights* (2 vols.) [P,A] | 2nd | Oxford University Press | 2010* |
| Harris, D.J., *et al.* | *Law of the European Convention on Human Rights* [S] | 2nd | Oxford University Press | 2009 |
| Lester of Herne Hill, Lord, Pannick, Lord, and Herberg, Javan | *Human Rights Law and Practice* [P,A] | 3rd | LexisNexis Butterworths | 2009 |
| Beatson, Jack., *et al.* | *Human Rights: Judicial Protection in the United Kingdom* [P,A] | | Sweet & Maxwell | 2008 |
| Gearty, Conor | *Civil Liberties* [S] | | Oxford University Press | 2007 |

## Noteworthy websites, blogs, etc.:

### BLOGS

- 1 Crown Office Row, UK Human Rights Blog (http://ukhumanrightsblog.com/)
- Antoine Buyse, ed., ECHR (European Convention on Human Rights and Fundamental Freedoms) (http://echrblog.blogspot.co.uk/)
- Oxford Human Rights Hub, Oxford Human Rights Hub (http://ohrh.law.ox.ac.uk/blog/)

# IMMIGRATION and NATIONALITY LAW

This hugely important area of law is controlled almost entirely by statute and is a responsibility of the Home Office, through three specific departments: Border Force (responsible for border control), UK Visas and Immigration, and Immigration Enforcement. There is also a considerable body of jurisprudence interpreting and applying the key statutes. The titles below deal with the particulars of British citizenship and the status of persons such as British subjects and protected persons and the rules surrounding immigration to the United Kingdom from other countries. The status of European nationals and the procedure for asylum-seekers (refugees) and the rights of such claimants are other significant areas of research.

Principal statutes include the British Nationality Act 1981, the Immigration Act 1971, the Immigration and Asylum Act 1999, and the Nationality, Immigration, and Asylum Act 2002.

*Related topic(s): ADMINISTRATIVE LAW; CONSTITUTIONAL LAW; EUROPEAN UNION LAW; HUMAN RIGHTS and CIVIL LIBERTIES; SOCIAL SECURITY and WELFARE LAW.*

| Author(s) | Title | Edition | Publisher | Year |
|---|---|---|---|---|
| McKee, Richard, ed. | *LexisNexis Butterworths Immigration Law* [P] | | LexisNexis Butterworths | LL |
| Browne, Kevin | *CLP Legal Practice Guide: Immigration Law 2016* [P] | | College of Law Publishing | Annual |
| Jackson, David, *et al.* | *Immigration Law and Practice* [P] | 5th | Bloomsbury Professional | 2016 |
| Macdonald, Ian A., Q.C., and Toal, Ronan | *Macdonald's Immigration Law & Practice* [P] | 9th | LexisNexis Butterworths | 2015* |
| Phelan, Margaret and Gillespie, James | *Immigration Law Handbook* [P] | 9th | Oxford University Press | 2015 |
| Symes, Mark and Jorro, Peter | *Immigration Appeals and Remedies Handbook* [P] | | Bloomsbury Professional | 2015 |
| Fransman, Laurie | *British Nationality Law* [P] | 3rd | Bloomsbury Professional | 2011 |
| Seddon, Duran | *JCWI Guide to the Points Based System* [P] | | JCWI (Joint Council for the Welfare of Immigrants) | 2011 |

| Author(s) | Title | Edition | Publisher | Year |
|---|---|---|---|---|
| Symes, Mark and Jorro, Peter | Asylum Law and Practice [P] | 2nd | Bloomsbury Professional | 2010 |
| Macdonald, Ian A., Q.C., *et al.* | *Blackstone's Guide to the Borders, Citizenship, and Immigration Act 2009* [P] | | Oxford University Press | 2009 |
| Sikand, Maya, ed. | *Blackstone's Guide to the Criminal Justice and Immigration Act 2008* [P] | | Oxford University Press | 2009 |
| Seddon, Duran | *Immigration, Nationality & Refugee Handbook 2006* [P] | 6th | JCWI (Joint Council for the Welfare of Immigrants) | 2006 |

## Noteworthy websites, blogs, etc.:

### WEBSITE

- LexisNexis, LexisWeb: Immigration (http://lexisweb.co.uk/groups/immigration/)

### BLOGS

- Davidson Morris (firm), Immigration Law (http://www.davidsonmorris.com/davidsonmorris-immigration-blog/)
- Colin Yeo, Free Movement (https://www.freemovement.org.uk/)

## INFORMATION TECHNOLOGY LAW

The title Information Technology Law is used as something of a catch-all for a range of subtopics which all in some way deal with activities which involve the use of a computer. Generally speaking, though, these works tend to deal with some or all of the following matters: computer crimes, such as hacking, spreading viruses, and storing and transmitting child pornography; data protection; electronic commerce; defamation; and intellectual property issues such as software patenting, content copyright, trade marks, and domain name allocation. This is an area of the law which is primarily informed by way of statutory provisions and European Community directives, but as computer use continues to become ever more ubiquitous it is quickly developing a robust body of instructive case law.

Relevant statutes include the Patents Act 1977, Data Protection Act 1984, Copyright, Designs, and Patents Act 1988, Computer Misuse Act 1990, the Electronic Communications Act 2000, and the Digital Economy Act 2010.

Important European directives include the Directive on Copyright in the Information Society, Data Protection Directive, Electronic Commerce Directive, Legal Protection of Databases Directive, and the Software Protection Directive.

*Related topic(s): COPYRIGHT; DATA PROTECTION; DESIGNS; FREEDOM of INFORMATION; INTELLECTUAL PROPERTY LAW; PATENTS; PRIVACY LAW.*

| Author(s) | Title | Edition | Publisher | Year |
|---|---|---|---|---|
| Saxby, Stephen, ed. | *Encyclopedia of Information Technology Law* [P] | | Sweet & Maxwell | LL |
| Rowland, Diane, Kohl, Uta, and Charlesworth, Andrew | *Information Technology Law* [S] | 5th | Routledge | 2016 |
| Lloyd, Ian J. | *Cyber Law in the UK* [P] | 2nd | Wolters Kluwer | 2014 |
| Lloyd, Ian J. | *Information Technology Law* [S] | 7th | Oxford University Press | 2014 |
| Murray, Andrew | *Information Technology Law: The Law and Society* [S] | 2nd | Oxford University Press | 2013 |
| Morgan, Richard and Burden, Kit | *Morgan & Burden on IT Contracts* [P] | 9th | Sweet & Maxwell | 2013 |

| Author(s) | Title | Edition | Publisher | Year |
|---|---|---|---|---|
| Phillips, Jeremy | LexisNexis Butterworths e-Commerce and IT Law Handbook [P] | 6th | LexisNexis Butterworths | 2012 |
| Reed, Chris, ed. | *Computer Law* [S] | 7th | Oxford University Press | 2011 |
| Davidson, Alan | *The Law of Electronic Commerce* [P,S] | | Cambridge University Press | 2010 |
| Bainbridge, David | *Introduction to Information Technology Law* [S] | 6th | Pearson Education | 2007 |
| Mason, Stephen | *E-Mail, Networks and the Internet: A Concise Guide to Compliance with the Law* [P] | | XPL Law | 2006 |

## Noteworthy websites, blogs, etc.:

### WEBSITE

- LexisNexis, Lexis Web: IP & IT (http://lexisweb.co.uk/groups/ip-it/default.aspx)

### BLOGS

- Amberhawk Associates, Hawktalk (http://amberhawk.typepad.com/amberhawk/)
- City University, Centre for Law, Justice, and Journalism Blog (https://blogs.city.ac.uk/cljj/)
- Fieldfisher (firm), Privacy and Information Law Blog (http://privacylawblog.fieldfisher.com/)
- Nick Holmes, Binary Law (www.binarylaw.co.uk)
- Information Commissioner's Office, ICO Blog (https://iconewsblog.wordpress.com/)
- International Forum for Responsible Media (Inforrm), Inforrm's BLOG Case Law (https://inforrm.wordpress.com/category/caselaw/)
- Mills & Reeve (firm), Technology Law Update (http://www.technology-law-blog.co.uk/)
- Olswang (firm), Datonomy: The Data Protection Blog (http://datonomy.eu/)
- Graham Smith, Cyberleagle (http://cyberleagle.blogspot.co.uk/)
- Tim Turner, 2040 Information Law Blog (http://2040infolawblog.com/)

# INSOLVENCY LAW

Often conjoined with bankruptcy, the term insolvency means the inability to pay debts whereas bankruptcy is the condition of having been deemed a bankrupt by a court. The titles listed here deal with both insolvency and bankruptcy.

Many of the works on this matter deal with the procedural aspects of bankruptcy actions which are enumerated primarily in the Insolvency Act 1986 (and 2000), some statutory instruments, and a number of practice directives in relation to bankruptcy proceedings.

The major topics within this title include bankruptcy court procedure, voluntary bankruptcies, bankruptcy actions by creditors, duties and powers of trustees in bankruptcy, the administration of a bankrupt's estate, and criminal bankruptcy.

Some insolvency law listings include titles dealing with the general legal relationship between debtors and creditors. It is not the case here as not all debtors are insolvent and not all creditors have initiated bankruptcy proceedings. Therefore for such titles, see DEBTOR & CREDITOR LAW.

*Related topic(s): COMMERCIAL LAW; DEBTOR & CREDITOR LAW; LOANS and MORTGAGES*

| Author(s) | Title | Edition | Publisher | Year |
|---|---|---|---|---|
| Briggs, John, Brougham, Chris, and Hunter, Muir | *Muir Hunter on Personal Insolvency* [P] | | Sweet & Maxwell | LL |
| Marks, David and Kaye, His Honour Judge Roger | *Tolley's Insolvency Law* [P] | | LexisNexis Butterworths | LL |
| Totty, Peter, Moss, Gabriel, and Segal, Nick, eds. | *Insolvency* [P] | | Sweet & Maxwell | LL |
| Davis, Glen and Haywood, Marcus, eds. | *LexisNexis Butterworths Insolvency Law Handbook 2016* [P] | 18th | LexisNexis Butterworths | Annual |
| Sealy, Len, Milman, David, and Bailey, Peter | *Sealy & Milman: Annotated Guide to the Insolvency Legislation 2015* [P] | 14th | Sweet & Maxwell | Annual |
| Frisby, Sandra, *et al.* | *Corporate Insolvency Law* [P,S] | | Oxford University Press | 2016 |

| Author(s) | Title | Edition | Publisher | Year |
|---|---|---|---|---|
| Insolvency Practitioners Association | *Insolvency Practitioners Handbook* [P] | 4th | LexisNexis Butterworths | 2015 |
| Levaggi, Peter and Elford, Roger | *Property Insolvency* [P] | 2nd | Jordan Publishing | 2015 |
| Bailey, Edward and Groves, Hugo | *Corporate Insolvency: Law and Practice* [P] | 4th | LexisNexis Butterworths | 2014 |
| Loose, Peter and Griffiths, Michael | *Loose & Griffiths on Liquidators* [P] | 8th | Jordan Publishing | 2014 |
| Dennis, Vernon | *Insolvency Law Handbook* [P] | 3rd | The Law Society | 2013 |
| Goode, Roy | *Principles of Corporate Insolvency Law* [P,A] | 4th | Sweet & Maxwell | 2011 |
| Calnan, Richard | *Proprietary Rights and Insolvency* [P] | | Oxford University Press | 2010 |
| Dennis, Vernon | *Administration* [P] | | The Law Society | 2010 |
| Ho, Look Chan and Smithson, Helen | *LexisNexis Butterworths Guide to the Insolvency Rules* [P] | | LexisNexis Butterworths | 2010 |
| Watson-Gandy, Mark | *Personal Insolvency Practice: Litigation, Procedure and Precedents* [P] | | Wildy, Simmonds & Hill | 2012 |
| Watson-Gandy, Mark | *Corporate Insolvency Practice: Litigation, Procedure and Precedents* [P] | | Wildy, Simmonds & Hill | 2010 |
| Mills, Simon, ed. | *Goode on Proprietary Rights and Insolvency in Sales Transactions* [P,A] | 3rd | Sweet & Maxwell | 2009 |
| Fletcher, Ian F. | *The Law of Insolvency* [P,A] | 4th | Sweet & Maxwell | 2009 |
| Frisby, Sandra, *et al.* | *Kerr & Hunter on Receivers and Administrators* [P,A] | 19th | Sweet & Maxwell | 2009 |
| Schaw Miller, Stephen and Bailey, Edward | *Personal Insolvency: Law and Practice* [P,A] | 4th | LexisNexis Butterworths | 2008 |

## Noteworthy websites, blogs, etc.:

### WEBSITES

- Jordan Publishing, Jordan's Insolvency Law: Latest Cases (http://www.jordanpublishing.co.uk/practice-areas/insolvency/news_and_comment?filter[category_id]=2751)

- LexisNexis, LexisWeb: Restructuring & Insolvency (http://lexisweb.co.uk/groups/restructuring-insolvency/default.aspx)

## BLOG

- LexisNexis, Restructuring and Insolvency (Randi) Blog (http://blogs.lexisnexis.co.uk/randi/)

# INSURANCE LAW

Insurance law is a specific subset of contract law with its own set of complex principles and rules. As a type of contract law it shares concepts such as formation of the contract, misrepresentation, *inter alia*. Matters specific to insurance law are those such as subrogation, certain types of indemnification, and reinsurance. There are many types of insurance such as property, life, health, motor vehicle, liability, accident and sickness, aviation, and marine insurance amongst others.

Important statutes include the Finance Act 1994, the Financial Services and Markets Act 2000, and the Marine Insurance Act 1906. Specific components of the topic are dealt with by the Third Parties (Rights Against Insurers) Act 2010 and the Consumer Insurance (Disclosure and Representations) Act 2012. Given that the law surrounding insurance is a type of contract law, jurisprudence remains a major source of authority for this topic.

*Related topic(s): CONTRACT LAW; MEDICAL LAW; NEGLIGENCE; ROAD TRAFFIC LAW; REAL PROPERTY; SHIPPING, TRANSORT, and MARITIME LAW; TORT LAW.*

| Author(s) | Title | Edition | Publisher | Year |
|---|---|---|---|---|
| Birds, John, *et al.* | *Encyclopedia of Insurance Law* [P] | | Sweet & Maxwell | LL |
| Clarke, Malcolm A. | *The Law of Insurance Contracts* [P] | | Informa | LL |
| Birds, John | *Birds' Modern Insurance Law* [S] | 10th | Sweet & Maxwell | 2016 |
| Barton, Andrew, ed. | *LexisNexis Butterworths Insurance Law Handbook* [P] | 14th | LexisNexis Butterworths | 2013 |
| Birds, John, Lynch, Ben, and Milnes, Simon | *MacGillivray on Insurance Law: Law Relating to All Risks Other than Marine* [P] | 13th | Sweet & Maxwell | 2015 |
| Gurses, Ozlem | *Marine Insurance Law* [P] | | Routledge | 2015 |
| Merkin, Robert | *Colinvaux's Law of Insurance* [P] | 10th | Sweet & Maxwell | 2015 |
| Merkin, Robert, Stuart-Smith, Jeremy | *The Law of Motor Insurance* [P] | 2nd | Sweet & Maxwell | 2015 |
| O'Neill, Terry and Woloniecki, Jan | *The Law of Reinsurance in England and Bermuda* [P] | 4th | Sweet & Maxwell | 2015 |

| Author(s) | Title | Edition | Publisher | Year |
|---|---|---|---|---|
| Lowry, John and Rawlings, Philip | *Insurance Law: Doctrines and Principles* [S] | 3rd | Hart Publishing | 2011 |
| Barlow Lyde & Gilbert LLP | *Insurance Law Handbook* [P] | 4th | Bloomsbury Professional | 2008 |
| Sherriff, Gerald | *Understanding Property Insurance* [P] | | The Law Society | 2008 |
| Mitchell, Charles and Watterson, Stephen | *Subrogation: Law and Practice* [P,A] | | Oxford University Press | 2007 |

## Noteworthy websites, blogs, etc.:

### WEBSITE

- Fraud Advisory Panel, Resources (https://www.fraudadvisorypanel.org/resource/)

# INTELLECTUAL PROPERTY LAW

The term 'intellectual property' is used generally as the legal category under which one finds works on copyright, databases, designs, patents, and trade marks. The titles listed hereunder are those which deal with all or most of the above topics in one title. There are concepts which are common to most categories of intellectual property such as assignment of rights, employee creations, moral rights, *inter alia*.

These subjects are based both in statutory and case law. Significant legislation includes: Copyright, Designs, and Patents Act 1988, Trade Marks Act 1994, Data Protection Act 1998.

The former Patents County Court has been renamed and repurposed as the Intellectual Property Enterprise Court which provides for a simpler process for disputes involving patents, copyright, trade marks, and designs.

*Related topic(s): COPYRIGHT; DATA PROTECTION; DESIGNS; FREEDOM of INFORMATION; INFORMATION TECHNOLOGY LAW; PATENTS; TELECOMMUNICATIONS LAW; TRADE MARKS.*

| Author(s) | Title | Edition | Publisher | Year |
|---|---|---|---|---|
| Denton Wilde Sapte LLP, ed. | *Practical Intellectual Property* [P] | | Sweet & Maxwell | LL |
| Galloway, Jonathan, *et al.* | *Modern Intellectual Property* [S] | 4th | Routledge | 2016 |
| Phillips, Jeremy | *Butterworths Intellectual Property Law Handbook* [P] | 12th | LexisNexis Butterworths | 2015 |
| Bently, Lionel and Sherman, Brad | *Intellectual Property Law* [S,P] | 4th | Oxford University Press | 2014 |
| Christie, Andrew and Gare, Stephen | *Blackstone's Statutes on Intellectual Property* [P,S] | 12th | Oxford University Press | 2014* |
| Fox, Angela | *The Intellectual Property Enterprise Court: Practice and Procedure* [P] | | Sweet & Maxwell | 2014 |
| Aplin, Tanya and Davis, Jennifer | *Intellectual Property Law: Text, Cases, and Materials* [S] | 2nd | Oxford University Press | 2013 |
| Balganesh, Shyamkrishna, ed. | *Intellectual Property and the Common Law* [A] | | Cambridge University Press | 2013 |
| Brazell, Lorna, ed. | *Intellectual Property Law Handbook* [P] | 2nd | The Law Society | 2013 |
| Cornish, William R. | *Intellectual Property:* | 8th | Sweet & Maxwell | 2013 |

| Author(s) | Title | Edition | Publisher | Year |
|---|---|---|---|---|
| Llewelyn, David, and Aplin, Tanya | *Patents, Copyright, Trade Marks, and Allied Rights* [S,P,A] | | | |
| Jacob, The Rt. Hon. Sir Robin, Alexander, Daniel, Q.C., and Fisher, Matthew | *A Guidebook to Intellectual Property: Patents, Trade Marks, Copyright and Designs* [S] | 6th | Sweet & Maxwell | 2013 |
| Torremans, David | *Holyoak & Torremans: Intellectual Property Law* [S] | 7th | Oxford University Press | 2013 |
| Garnett, Kevin and Davies, Gillian | *Moral Rights* [P,A] | | Sweet & Maxwell | 2010 |

## Noteworthy websites, blogs, etc.:

### WEBSITE

- LexisNexis, Lexis Web: IP & IT (http://lexisweb.co.uk/groups/ip-it/default.aspx)

### BLOGS

- Mark Anderson, IP Draughts (https://ipdraughts.wordpress.com/)
- Fieldfisher (firm), Intellectual Property Blog (http://intellectualpropertyblog.fieldfisher.com/)
- LexisNexis, World of IP and IT (WIPIT) Blog (http://blogs.lexisnexis.co.uk/wipit/)
- Shireen Smith, Azrights News and Media (www.venables.co.uk/blogs.htm)
- Neil J. Wilkof, et al., The IPKat (www.ipkat.com)

# INTERNATIONAL CRIMINAL LAW

A modern definition of international criminal law refers to sanctions against heinous crimes and atrocities such as genocide, war crimes, and crimes against humanity examples of which are the actions against the perpetrators of genocide in Rwanda and 'ethnic cleansing' in the former Yugoslavia. A number of such matters will be adjudicated by the International Criminal Court in The Hague, Netherlands.

Earlier definitions of the topic deal with counter-terrorism activities and matters involving United Kingdom citizens and residents and the commission of crimes in other nations or those committed by foreign nationals in the United Kingdom. Extradition to and from the United Kingdom is an important topic within this subject.

*Related topic(s): CRIMINAL LAW; HUMAN RIGHTS and CIVIL LIBERTIES; IMMIGRATION and NATIONALITY LAW; INTERNATIONAL LAW; PRACTICE & PROCEDURE (CRIMINAL).*

| Author(s) | Title | Edition | Publisher | Year |
|---|---|---|---|---|
| Jones, John R.W.D. and Zgonec-Rozej, Misa, eds. | *Blackstone's International Criminal Practice* [P] | | Oxford University Press | 2016 |
| O'Keefe, Roger | *International Criminal Law* [S,A] | | Oxford University Press | 2015 |
| Schabas, William | *The Cambridge Companion to International Criminal Law* [A] | | Cambridge University Press | 2015 |
| Stahn, Carsten, ed. | *The Law and Practice of the International Criminal Court* [P,A] | | Oxford University Press | 2015 |
| Cryer, Robert, *et al.* | *An Introduction to International Criminal Law and Procedure* [S,P] | 3rd | Cambridge University Press | 2014 |
| Dixon, Rodney and Khan, Karim A.A. | *Archbold International Criminal Courts: Practice, Procedure & Evidence* [P] | 4th | Sweet & Maxwell | 2014 |
| Nicholls, Clive, *et al.* | *Nicholls, Montgomery, and Knowles on the Law of Extradition and Mutual Assistance* [P] | 3rd | Oxford University Press | 2013 |

| Author(s) | Title | Edition | Publisher | Year |
|---|---|---|---|---|
| Sluiter, Goran, *et al.*, eds. | *International Criminal Procedure: Principles and Rules* [P] | | Oxford University Press | 2013 |
| Natarajan, Mangai | *International Crime and Justice* [A] | | Cambridge University Press | 2012 |
| Cassese, Antonio, *et al.* | *International Criminal Law: Cases and Commentary* [S] | | Oxford University Press | 2011 |
| Schabas, William | *An Introduction to the International Criminal Court* [S,P,A] | 4th | Cambridge University Press | 2011 |
| Bantekas, Ilias | *International Criminal Law* [S] | 4th | Hart Publishing | 2010 |
| Bellelli, Roberto, ed. | *International Criminal Justice: Law and Practice from the Rome Statute to its Review* [A] | | Ashgate | 2010 |
| Jones, R.W.D. and Davidson, Rosemary | *Extradition and Mutual Legal Assistance Handbook* [P] | 2nd | Oxford University Press | 2010 |
| Cassese, Antonio, ed. | *The Oxford Companion to International Criminal Justice* [A] | | Oxford University Press | 2009 |
| Sambei, Arvinder, du Plessis, Anton, and Polaine, Martin | *Counter-Terrorism Law and Practice: An International Handbook* [P,A] | | Oxford University Press | 2009 |

# INTERNATIONAL INVESTMENT LAW

The law of international investing is a specific subset of public international law and is grounded almost entirely in numerous multilateral and bilateral treaties to which the United Kingdom is a signatory. The overarching intention of these treaties is to ensure that foreign investors enjoy the same protections for their investments as would citizen investors in the country hosting their investments. Many of these treaties are called Investment Promotion and Protection Agreements and are generally referred to as 'IPPAs'.

IPPAs provide a wide range of mechanisms which ensure fair and equitable treatment of the investor, the freedom of transfer (i.e., the ability to remove investments from the host country), and provide for dispute resolution and arbitration.

*Related topic(s): INTERNATIONAL LAW; INTERNATIONAL TRADE LAW.*

| Author(s) | Title | Edition | Publisher | Year |
|---|---|---|---|---|
| Bjorklund, Andrea K. and Newcombe, Andrew Paul | *International Investment Law and Arbitration: Cases, Materials, and Commentary* [S,A] | | Oxford University Press | 2016 |
| McLachlan, Campbell, Shore, Lawrence, and Weiniger, Matthew | *International Investment Arbitration: Substantive Principles* [S,P] | 2nd | Oxford University Press | 2016 |
| Salacuse, Jeswald W. | *The Law of Investment Treaties* [P,A] | 2nd | Oxford University Press | 2015 |
| Douglas, Zachary | *The International Law of Investment Claims* [P] | | Cambridge University Press | 2012 |
| Dolzer, Rudolph and Schruer, Christoph | *Principles of International Investment Law* [P,A] | 2nd | Oxford University Press | 2012 |
| Webster, Thomas H. | *Handbook of Investment Arbitration: Commentary, Precedents, and Models for ICSID Arbitration* [P] | | Sweet & Maxwell | 2012 |
| Sornarajah, M. | *The International Law on Foreign Investment* [S,P] | 3rd | Cambridge University Press | 2010 |

| Author(s) | Title | Edition | Publisher | Year |
|---|---|---|---|---|
| Muchlinski, Peter, Ortino, Federico, and Schreuer, Christoph | Oxford Handbook of International Investment Law [A] | | Oxford University Press | 2008 |

# INTERNATIONAL LAW

There are two principal streams of international law: public and private. Public international law deals with the legal relationships between independent nation states either individually or in aggregations with other states. Private international law deals with private individuals (or groups of individuals) and their private legal interactions with foreign nation states. Frequently the legal matters involved in private international law are basically conflict of laws problems. Most of the works listed under this title deal exclusively with public international law and the numerous international treaties to which the United Kingdom and European Union are signatories.

*Related topic(s): AIR and SPACE LAW; CONFLICT of LAWS; EUROPEAN UNION LAW; HUMAN RIGHTS and CIVIL LIBERTIES; INTERNATIONAL CRIMINAL LAW; INTERNATIONAL INVESTMENT LAW; INTERNATIONAL TRADE LAW; SHIPPING, TRANSPORT, and MARITIME LAW; TELECOMMUNICATIONS LAW.*

| **Author(s)** | **Title** | **Edition** | **Publisher** | **Year** |
|---|---|---|---|---|
| Rothwell, Don and Stephens, Tim | *The International Law of the Sea* [S] | 2nd | Hart Publishing | 2016 |
| Kaczorowska-Ireland, Alina | *Public International Law* [S] | 5th | Routledge | 2015 |
| Lowe, Vaughan | *International Law: A Very Short Introduction* [S] | | Oxford University Press | 2015 |
| Ryngaert, Cedric | *Jurisdiction in International Law* [A] | 2nd | Oxford University Press | 2015 |
| Fleck, Dieter, ed. | *The Handbook of International Humanitarian Law* [A] | 3rd | Oxford University Press | 2014 |
| Shaw, Malcolm N. | *International Law* [S,P,A] | 7th | Cambridge University Press | 2014 |
| Aust, Anthony | *Modern Treaty Law and Practice* [S,A] | 3rd | Cambridge University Press | 2013 |
| Dixon, Martin | *Textbook on International Law* [S] | 7th | Oxford University Press | 2013 |
| Lepard, Brian D. | *Customary International Law: A New Theory with Practical Applications* [A] | | Cambridge University Press | 2010 |
| Aust, Anthony | *Handbook of International Law* [S,P] | 2nd | Cambridge University Press | 2010 |

| Author(s) | Title | Edition | Publisher | Year |
|---|---|---|---|---|
| Henderson, Conway W. | *Understanding International Law* [S] | | Wiley-Blackwell | 2010 |
| Sammut, Mark | *The Law of Consular Relations* [P] | | XPL Law | 2010 |
| Evans, Malcolm and Capps, Patrick | *International Law* (2 volumes) [A] | | Ashgate | 2009 |
| Brownlie, Ian and Goodwin-Gill, Guy S., eds. | *Brownlie's Documents on International Law* [S] | 6th | Oxford University Press | 2010 |
| Brownlie, Ian | *Principles of Public International Law* [S,P] | 7th | Oxford University Press | 2008 |

## Noteworthy websites, blogs, etc.:

### WEBSITES

- Journal of Private International Law, Conflict of Laws.net (http://conflictoflaws.net/)

# INTERNATIONAL TRADE LAW

International trade law is usually defined as the branch of public international law that addresses measures that states may take with respect to the international movement of goods, services, investments, and workers. It includes the rules contained in global agreements, including the WTO treaties, regional trade agreements and bilateral treaties. European Union law includes many rules on cross-border trade, but EU law is now considered a distinct branch of law in its own right. Normally this topic does not comprise works dealing with the law of doing business in other jurisdictions, but for the purposes of this work, such international commercial law titles are included.

One domestic component of international trade law is that of Customs and Excise which are grounded largely in numerous statutory instruments. Prior to 2005, Her Majesty's Customs and Excise was an independent government department; however, it is now a constituent part of HM Revenue and Customs.

*Related topic(s): INTERNATIONAL INVESTMENT LAW; INTERNATIONAL LAW.*

| Author(s) | Title | Edition | Publisher | Year |
|---|---|---|---|---|
| Kritzer, Albert H., *et al.* | *International Contract Manual* [P] | | Sweet & Maxwell | LL |
| Bamford, Colin | *Principles of International Financial Law* [P,A] | 2nd | Oxford University Press | 2015 |
| Bhala, Raj | *Modern GATT Law: A Treatise on the Law and Political Economy of the GATT* (2 vols.) [A,P] | 2nd | Sweet & Maxwell | 2013 |
| Bridge, Michael | *The International Sale of Goods: Law and Practice* [P,A] | 3rd | Oxford University Press | 2013 |
| Carr, Indira | *International Trade* [S] | 5th | Routledge | 2013 |
| Chuah, Jason C.T. | *Law of International Trade: Cross Border Commercial Transactions* [S] | 5th | Sweet & Maxwell | 2013 |
| Murray, Carole, Holloway, David, and Timson-Hunt, Daren | *Schmitthoff: The Law and Practice of International Trade* [P] | 12th | Sweet & Maxwell | 2012 |

| Author(s) | Title | Edition | Publisher | Year |
|---|---|---|---|---|
| Leal-Arcas, Rafael | International Trade and Investment Law: Multi-lateral, Regional and Bilateral Governance [P] | | Edward Elgar | 2010 |
| Bethlehem, Daniel, *et al.* | *Oxford Handbook of International Trade Law* [A] | | Oxford University Press | 2009 |
| Inama, Stefano | *Rules of Origin in International Trade* [A] | | Cambridge University Press | 2009 |

## Noteworthy websites, blogs, etc.:

### WEBSITE

- CMP Publishing, International Trade & Economic Law (http://www.cmppublishing.com/economic-law.html)

# LANDLORD and TENANT LAW

The titles listed under this topic deal with rented property in all contexts other than that of residential rentals. Most of these works deal with commercial or agricultural tenancies. For works related to the rental of residential properties, see RESIDENTIAL TENANCIES.

Themes which are commonly dealt with under this topic include the relationship of landlord and tenant and the duties and obligations of each, the specifics of lease agreements, covenants, and the assignment of tenancy agreements.

This area of law has its roots in antiquity and as such there is an enormous body of jurisprudence articulating its major principles, however there are also a few legislative enactments of note, such as the Common and Leasehold Reform Act 2002, the Landlord and Tenant Act 1927, 1954, 1985, and 1987, the Landlord and Tenant (Covenant) Act 1995, the Law of Property Act 1925, and the Leasehold Reform Act 1967.

*Related topic(s): AGRICULTURAL LAW; HOUSING LAW; REAL PROPERTY; RESIDENTIAL TENANCIES LAW.*

| Author(s) | Title | Edition | Publisher | Year |
|---|---|---|---|---|
| Aldridge, Trevor M. | *Leasehold Law* [P] | | Sweet & Maxwell | LL |
| Lewison, The Rt. Hon. Mr. Justice | *Woodfall: Landlord & Tenant* [P] | | Sweet & Maxwell | LL |
| Furber, John and Moss, Joanne R., eds. | *Hill & Redman's Law of Landlord and Tenant* [P] | | LexisNexis Butterworths | LL |
| Radevsky, Anthony and Greenish, Damian | *Hague on Leasehold Enfranchisement* [P,A] | 6th | Sweet & Maxwell | 2014* |
| Webber, Gary and Dovar, Daniel | *Business Premises: Possession and Lease Renewal* [P] | 5th | Sweet & Maxwell | 2014 |
| Garner, Simon and Frith, Alexandra | *A Practical Approach to Landlord and Tenant* [S,P] | 7th | Oxford University Press | 2013 |
| Bradford, Katie and Matthews, Paul, eds. | *Butterworths Business Landlord and Tenant Handbook* [P] | 6th | LexisNexis Butterworths | 2012 |

| Author(s) | Title | Edition | Publisher | Year |
|---|---|---|---|---|
| Sydenham, Angela | *Agricultural Tenancies* [P] | 2nd | Wildy, Simmonds & Hill | 2009 |
| Hanbury, William | *Defective Premises: Law and Practice* [P] | | Sweet & Maxwell | 2008 |
| Reynolds, Kirk and Clark, Wayne | *Reynolds & Clarke: Renewal of Business Tenancies* [P] | 4th | Sweet & Maxwell | 2007* |

## Noteworthy websites, blogs, etc.:

### BLOGS

- Clutton Cox (firm), Landlord and tenant blog (http://www.cluttoncox.co.uk/site/blog/landlordandtenantblog/)
- PainSmith Solicitors, PainSmith Landlord and Tenant blog (https://blog.painsmith.co.uk/)
- Tessa Shepperson, The Landlord Law Blog (http://www.landlordlawblog.co.uk/)
- The Landlord Law BLOG Case Reports (http://www.landlordlawblog.co.uk/category/law-case-report/)

# LEGAL SKILLS and METHOD

Practitioners of the law need to master a suite of competencies, particularly legal research, writing, reasoning, drafting (e.g., agreements, pleadings, etc.), as well as negotiation and client counselling. Listed here are works which endeavour to instruct in these various skills. Many of them also impart basic information about the workings of the legal system. While such works are found in all countries, these titles are specifically British.

For titles specific to writing and drafting, see DRAFTING and LEGAL WRITING.

*Related topic(s): ADVOCACY; ARBITRATION and DISPUTE RESOLUTION; ENGLISH LEGAL SYSTEM; STATUTORY INTERPRETATION and LEGISLATIVE DRAFTING.*

| Author(s) | Title | Edition | Publisher | Year |
|---|---|---|---|---|
| Finch, Emily and Fafinski, Stefan | *Legal Skills* [S] | 5th | Oxford University Press | 2015 |
| Haigh, Rupert | *Legal English* [S,P] | 4th | Routledge | 2015 |
| Hanson, Sharon | *Learning Legal Skills and Reasoning* [S] | 3rd | Routledge | 2015 |
| Higgins, Edwina and Tatham, Laura | *Successful Legal Writing* [S] | 3rd | Sweet & Maxwell | 2015 |
| Slorach, Scott, *et al.* | *Legal Systems & Skills* [S] | 2nd | Oxford University Press | 2015 |
| Clinch, Peter and Beaumont, Jon | *Legal Research: A Practi-tioner's Handbook* [P,S] | 2nd | Wildy, Simmonds & Hill | 2013 |
| McLeod, Ian | *Palgrave Law Masters: Legal Method* [S] | 9th | Palgrave Macmillan | 2013 |
| Smith, A.T.H. | *Glanville Williams: Learning the Law* [P,N] | 15th | Sweet & Maxwell | 2013 |
| Knowles, John and Thomas, Philip | *Effective Legal Research* [S] | 3rd | Sweet & Maxwell | 2012 |
| Stychin, Carl F. and Mulcahy, Linda | *Legal Method and Systems: Text and Materials* [S] | 4th | Sweet & Maxwell | 2010 |
| Twining, William and Miers, David | *Law in Context: How to do Things with Rules* [S,A] | 5th | Cambridge University Press | 2010 |
| Boyle, Fiona, *et al.* | *A Practical Guide to Lawyering Skills* [S] | 3rd | Routledge-Cavendish | 2005 |

| Author(s) | Title | Edition | Publisher | Year |
|---|---|---|---|---|
| Maughan, Caroline and Webb, Julian | *Lawyering Skills and the Legal Process* [S] | 2nd | Cambridge University Press | 2005 |

## Noteworthy websites, blogs, etc.:

### BLOG

- Nick Holmes, Binary Law (www.binarylaw.co.uk)

# LIBEL and SLANDER

The specific tort of defamation (libel if in writing; slander if spoken) creates a cause of action when statements are made which bring one's reputation into doubt. Libellous statements are actionable whereas slanderous ones are only so if actual damage can be proven, unless the statement is one which imputes that the plaintiff committed a criminal offence or tends to call into question the plaintiff's professional competence.

This area of law is grounded largely in the common law but a key statute is the Defamation Act 1996 which was partially reformed by the Defamation Act 2013, the intent of which is to impose more stringent requirements upon plaintiffs and reduce the number of vexatious and frivolous defamation actions.

In rare circumstances, defamation can be found to be criminal in addition to being tortious. It is only under a criminal action for defamation that the defaming of a dead person can be pursued.

Important sub-issues include determining what constitutes a defamatory statement, defences, such as the truth and privilege (absolute or qualified), and fair comment.

Malicious falsehoods—lies intended to cause harm—are not pursued under this legal heading but numerous libel and slander works touch upon this topic.

*Related topic(s): CRIMINAL LAW; MEDIA and ENTERTAINMENT LAW; PRIVACY LAW; TORT LAW.*

| Author(s) | Title | Edition | Publisher | Year |
|---|---|---|---|---|
| Mullis, Alistair, Parkes, Richard, and Busuttil, Godwin, eds. | *Gatley on Libel and Slander* [P,A] | 12th | Sweet & Maxwell | 2015 |
| Neill, Sir Brian, *et al.* | *Duncan and Neill on Defamation* [P,A] | 4th | LexisNexis Butterworths | 2015 |
| Collins, Matthew | *Collins on Defamation* [P,A] | | Oxford University Press | 2014 |
| Price, James and McMahon, Felicity, eds. | *Blackstone's Guide to the Defamation Act 2013* [S,P] | | Oxford University Press | 2013 |
| Collins, Matthew | *The Law of Defamation and the Internet* [P,A] | 3rd | Oxford University Press | 2011 |

| Author(s) | Title | Edition | Publisher | Year |
|---|---|---|---|---|
| Doley, Cameron and Mullis, Alistair, eds. | Carter-Ruck on Libel and Privacy [P,A] | 6th | LexisNexis Butterworths | 2010 |
| Price, David, Duodu, Korieh, and Cain, Nicola | *Defamation: Law, Procedure and Practice* [P] | 4th | Sweet & Maxwell | 2009 |
| Milo, Dario | *Defamation and Freedom of Speech* [A] | | Oxford University Press | 2008 |

## Noteworthy websites, blogs, etc.:

### WEBSITES

- Carruthers Law (firm), (http://www.carruthers-law.co.uk/news-articles/#.Vs8iyZwrK71)

# LICENSING LAW

Certain commercial activities are subject to powers exercised by the Secretary of State for Culture, Media and Sport by way of the Licensing Act 2003. Licensed activities relate primarily to gambling (for titles, see GAMING & LOTTERIES), the sale and consumption of alcohol, and various types of public entertainment.

With regard to alcohol licensing, issues include premises licences, club premises, temporary and special events, and personal licences. The rights and responsibilities of innkeepers and hoteliers are also dealt with in these titles.

As far as entertainment is concerned, licensing law deals with theatres, cinemas, the content of some video recordings, plays, raves, demonstrations of hypnotism, and sex establishments (both venues for public performances and sex shops). Some activities are governed by their own specific statute, e.g., Films Act 1985, Theatres Act 1968, and Video Recordings Act 1984.

For licensing of taxis and minicabs, see ROAD TRAFFIC LAW.

*Related topic(s): CRIMINAL LAW; GAMING & LOTTERIES; LOCAL GOVERNMENT LAW; MEDIA and ENTERTAINMENT LAW.*

| Author(s) | Title | Edition | Publisher | Year |
|---|---|---|---|---|
| Hyde, Philip | *Licensing Procedures and Precedents* [P] | | Sweet & Maxwell | LL |
| Phillips, Jeremy, *et al.*, eds. | *Paterson's Licensing Acts 2016* [P] | | LexisNexis Butterworths | Annual |
| Hewitson, Russell | *Licensing Law Handbook: A Practical Guide to Liquor and Entertainment Licensing* [P] | 2nd | The Law Society | 2013 |
| Kolvin, Philip | *Licensed Premises Law: Practice and Policy* [P] | 2nd | Bloomsbury Professional | 2013 |
| Ashton, David and Reid, Paul W. | *Ashton & Reid on Clubs and Associations* [P] | 2nd | Jordan Publishing | 2011 |
| Barker, Kerry and Stevens, Henry | *Club Law Manual* [P] | 2nd | Wildy, Simmonds & Hill | 2011 |
| Hyde, Philip and Rohsler, Carl | *Licensing Law and Practice* [P] | | Sweet & Maxwell | 2008 |

| Author(s) | Title | Edition | Publisher | Year |
|---|---|---|---|---|
| Manchester, Colin, Poppleston, Susanna, and Allen, Jeremy | *Alcohol and Entertainment Licensing Law* [P,S] | 2nd | Routledge-Cavendish | 2008 |
| Pain, Kenneth W. and Pain, Kevin M. | *Licensing Practice and Procedure* [P] | 9th | Callow Publishing | 2008 |

## Noteworthy websites, blogs, etc.:

### WEBSITES

- Poppleston Allen (firm), (http://www.popall.co.uk/)

# LIMITATION

A 'limitation' is the period within which an action must be commenced. This requirement exists to improve fairness in all proceedings by helping to ensure the reliability and freshness of evidence and testimony. For differing types of actions there is a range of limitation periods in play.

For the most part reference is made to the Limitation Act 1980 which articulates a number of different limitation periods depending on the type of claim being brought forward. There are also some Acts which set specific limitation periods for actions brought under their authority. For example the Employment Rights Act 1996 deals with actions before an employment tribunal. In cases where a specific Act details a limitation period the Limitation Act 1980 does not apply. In most other cases, however, the Act is applicable but with a few exceptions such as actions involving the Crown and probate proceedings *inter alia*.

This is an area of research based solidly in statute law but there is a sizable body of case law interpreting these statutes and dealing with issues such as determining when the clock begins to run, the effects of fraud and concealment, and how to deal with foreign actions. This latter matter is also subject to statutory treatment by way of the Foreign Limitations Periods Act 1984.

*Related topic(s): PRACTICE & PROCEDURE (CIVIL).*

| Author(s) | Title | Edition | Publisher | Year |
|---|---|---|---|---|
| di Mambro, David, ed. | *Law of Limitation* [P] | | Bloomsbury Professional | LL |
| McGee, Andrew | *Limitation Periods* [P] | 7th | Sweet & Maxwell | 2015* |
| Canny, Martin | *Limitation of Actions in England and Wales* [P] | | Bloomsbury Professional | 2013 |
| Nelson-Jones, Rodney and Burton, Frank | *Personal Injury Limitation* [P] | 2nd | Bloomsbury Professional | 2007 |
| Prime, Terence and Scanlan, Gary | *The Law of Limitation* [P] | 2nd | Oxford University Press | 2001 |
| Oughton, D.W., Lowry, J.P., and Merkin, Robert M. | *Limitation of Actions* [P] | | Informa | 1998 |

## LOANS and MORTGAGES

These titles deal with either the law as it relates to loans of money or to the more complex matter of mortgages. A loan of money normally creates a loan contract and generally speaking the fundamentals of contract law, with a few deviations, apply thereto. It is important to note that a loan of money does not create an obligation but rather a debt. To secure a loan one might use any of the following: chattels, land, mortgages, debentures, stocks, insurance policies, and other such financial instruments. One might also pledge or pawn items as security.

While to most people a mortgage is simply a loan taken out to enable them to purchase property, it is a more complex device than that. A mortgage is essentially a debt secured by land or property of some type. There are legal mortgages (which can be created by demise or sub-demise) and equitable mortgages (created by a specific mortgage contract which since 1989 must be in writing).

There are common sub-topics within the mortgages heading including the creation of mortgages, the parties to a mortgage, priority of mortgages, redemption, the rights and responsibilities of mortgagors (borrowers) and mortgagees (lenders), including remedies available to them, and the discharge of mortgages.

This is a long standing area of law based largely in case law. The most pertinent statute, however, is the Law of Property Act 1925 (particularly Part III).

*Related topic(s): BANKING and FINANCE LAW; BILLS of EXCHANGE and LETTERS of CREDIT; COMMERCIAL LAW; CONSTRUCTION LAW; CONTRACT LAW; CRIMINAL LAW; DEBTOR & CREDITOR LAW; EQUITY & TRUSTS; HOUSING LAW; INSOLVENCY LAW; LANDLORD and TENANT LAW; PROPERTY LAW; REAL PROPERTY; RESIDENTIAL TENANCIES LAW; SECURITIES.*

| Author(s) | Title | Edition | Publisher | Year |
|---|---|---|---|---|
| Burgess, Robert and Straun, Scott | *Law of Loans and Borrowing* [P] | | Sweet & Maxwell | LL |
| Hardwick, Richard, Lawrence, Jonathan, and Talbot, Richard, eds. | *Practical Lending and Security Precedents* [P] | | Sweet & Maxwell | LL |
| Cousins, Edward and Clarke, Ian | *Cousins on the Law of Mortgages* [P,A] | 4th | Sweet & Maxwell | 2016 |
| Fuller, Geoffrey | *Corporate Borrowing: Law and Practice* [P] | 5th | Jordan Publishing | 2016 |

| Author(s) | Title | Edition | Publisher | Year |
|---|---|---|---|---|
| Luba, Jan, *et al.* | *Defending Possession Proceedings* [P] | 8th | Legal Action Group | 2016 |
| Clark, Wayne, ed. | *Fisher and Lightwood's Law of Mortgage* [P,A] | 14th | LexisNexis Butterworths | 2014* |
| Webber, Gary and Dovar, Daniel | *Residential Possession Proceedings* [P] | 9th | Sweet & Maxwell | 2013 |
| Cummings, Christopher | *Practitioner's Guide to Mortgage Regulation* [P] | | City & Financial Publishing | 2007 |

## LOCAL GOVERNMENT LAW

The system of local government in England dates back to years prior to the Norman Conquest and has since developed in a seemingly haphazard manner resulting in a particularly complex and confusing patchwork of varying types of local authorities. A major revision of local government was achieved by the administration of Prime Minister Edward Heath by way of the Local Government Act 1972 (whose provisions took effect in 1974) which not only restricted local authorities but also abolished many resulting in the legal "disappearance" of a few counties such as Westmorland and Cumberland to name but two.

The English system of local government is complicated by the existence of differing types of local authorities with differing powers. There are metropolitan and non-metropolitan county councils and similarly there are metropolitan and non-metropolitan district councils plus the Greater London Authority as well as the thirty-two London borough councils, the City of London, and the local parish councils throughout England.

Generally speaking, some local governments can be termed "upper tier" authorities while others are "lower tier", the former normally taking responsibility for less mundane functions like education, libraries, social services, and strategic planning while the latter undertake such matters as waste collection, cemeteries, and licensing *inter alia*. Confusing matters more is the fact that there are also unitary authorities which undertake both levels of activities. Numerous new unitary authorities were created in 2009 out of non-metropolitan districts which were subsequently abolished.

All powers of local government are of course delegated by Parliament and no local authority is empowered to undertake any activity which it has not specifically been granted by way of Parliamentary enactment. The key statutes in this area are the various enactments of the Local Government Act. The most current is the Local Government Act 2003 but many sections of the earlier iterations of 1972, 1974, and 2000 remain in effect.

*Related topic(s): ADMINISTRATIVE LAW; CONSTITUTIONAL LAW; CONSTRUCTION LAW; ENVIRONMENTAL LAW; LICENSING; NUISANCE; PLANNING LAW; REAL PROPERTY; ROAD TRAFFIC LAW; SOCIAL SECURITY and WELFARE LAW; TAXATION.*

| Author(s) | Title | Edition | Publisher | Year |
|---|---|---|---|---|
| | *Encyclopedia of Local Government Law* [P] | | Sweet & Maxwell | LL |
| Aisbett, Alan, Grace, Clive, and Harrison, Alan, eds. | *Local Government Precedents and Procedures* [P] | | Sweet & Maxwell | LL |
| Cross, C.A. | *Cross on Local Government Law* [P] | | Sweet & Maxwell | LL |
| Hann, Robert | *Local Authority Companies & Partnerships* [P] | | Hann Barton | LL |
| Booth, Cherie Q.C. and Squires, Daniel | *The Negligence Liability of Public Authorities* [P,A] | 2nd | Oxford University Press | 2016 |
| Clayden, Paul | *Arnold-Baker on Local Council Administration* [P] | 9th | LexisNexis Butterworths | 2016 |
| Nicholls, Colin, Q.C., *et al.* | *Corruption and Misuse of Public Office* [P,A] | 3rd | Oxford University Press | 2016 |
| Randall, Helen, ed. | *Local Government Contracts and Procurement* | 3rd | Oxford University Press | 2016 |
| Morrell, John and Foster, His Honour Judge Richard Foster | *Local Authority Liability* [P] | 6th | Jordan Publishing | 2015 |
| Travers, David, Q.C., Grant, Edward, and Lambert, Emmaline | *Planning Enforcement* [P] | | Wildy, Simmonds & Hill | 2015 |
| Travers, David, Q.C., Byrd, Noemi, Atkinson, Giles | *Planning Law and Practice* [P] | | Wildy, Simmonds & Hill | 2013 |
| Norris, Julie and Phillips, Jeremy | *Law of Regulatory Enforcement and Sanctions: A Practical Guide* [P] | | Oxford University Press | 2011 |
| Clayden, Paul | *Local Council Clerk's Guide* [N] | 3rd | Sweet & Maxwell | 2010 |
| Clayden, Paul | *Law of Parks and Open Spaces* [P] | | Shaw & Sons | 2009 |
| Arden, Andrew | *Local Government Constitutional and Administrative Law* [P,A] | 2nd | Sweet & Maxwell | 2008 |

| Author(s) | Title | Edition | Publisher | Year |
|---|---|---|---|---|
| Sharland, John | *A Practical Approach to Local Government Law* [P,S] | 2nd | Oxford University Press | 2006 |

## Noteworthy websites, blogs, etc.:

### WEBSITE

- LexisNexis, Lexis Web: Local Government (http://lexisweb.co.uk/groups/local-government/default.aspx)

# MARRIAGE and CIVIL PARTNERSHIPS

These titles are works which deal with the establishment and the dissolution of matrimonial relationships. Until December of 2004 with the coming-into-force of the Civil Partnership Act 2004 such relationships were open only to a man and a woman and were governed by the Marriage Act 1949. The Civil Partnership Act 2004 afforded same sex couples the same rights and legal status as that of married couples. Since the passage of the Marriage (Same Sex Couples) Act 2013 two people of the same gender may be lawfully married. Moreover, those couples who had entered into a lawful civil partnership—whether in the UK or elsewhere—may convert their civil partnership into a marriage. It is important to note that it is not mandatory that civil partnerships be converted to marriages and that same-sex couples continue to be able to choose to enter into marriage or civil partnership.

The requirements for a valid marriage or civil partnership are essentially the same: that the parties be of age and have the mental capacity to marry, that neither party is already married or in a civil partnership, that the parties are not related to a prohibited degree, and that certain forms and ceremonies have been followed.

Marriages and civil partnerships come to end by way of death of one of the partners, by way of a marital cause (in the case of a marriage) or a civil partnership cause. Marital causes are divorce, nullity of marriage, or judicial separation while a civil partnership cause is one of is dissolution, annulment, or legal separation.

For the legal consequences of the breakdown of marriage or civil partnership, see FAMILY LAW.

*Related topic(s): CHILDREN; ECCLESIASTICAL LAW; FAMILY LAW; PROPERTY LAW.*

| Author(s) | Title | Edition | Publisher | Year |
|---|---|---|---|---|
| Everall, Mark, *et al.* | *Rayden and Jackson on Divorce and Family Matters* [P] | 18th | LexisNexis Butterworths | LL |
| Barker, Nicola and Monk, Daniel, eds. | *From Civil Partnership to Same-Sex Marriage* [A] | | Routledge | 2016 |
| Harper, Mark, *et al.* | *Same Sex Marriage and Civil Partnerships: The New Law* [P] | | Family Law | 2014 |
| Heaton, Clive, McCallum, Louise, and Jogi, Razia | *Forced Marriage: A Special Bulletin* [P] | | Jordan Publishing | 2009 |

| Author(s) | Title | Edition | Publisher | Year |
|---|---|---|---|---|
| Gray, Nichola and Brazil, Dominic | *Blackstone's Guide to The Civil Partnership Act 2004* [P] | | Oxford University Press | 2005 |
| Mallender, Paul and Rayson, Jane | *The Civil Partnership Act 2004* [P] | | Cambridge University Press | 2005 |

## Noteworthy websites, blogs, etc.:

### BLOGS

- Diane Benussi, Family Law Blog (http://www.benussilaw.co.uk/category/family-law-blog/)
- Lynne Halford, Divorce Solicitor (http://divorcesolicitor.blogspot.co.uk/)
- LexisNexis, Family Law Blog (http://blogs.lexisnexis.co.uk/family/)
- Jo Spain, Family Law Matters (http://www.spainwilliams.com/family/)

# MEDIA and ENTERTAINMENT LAW

These titles deal with many aspects of the law as it relates to the information and entertainment industries: television and radio, film, theatre, music, and publishing. These are areas grounded primarily in statutory law, including numerous statutory instruments, but there is also a large body of instructive case law. Much of the material written in this area deals with broadcasting which through OFCOM (the Office of Communications) is a heavily regulated activity.

A number of these works deal with other legal subjects in the context of media and entertainment law such as agency, contracts, and intellectual property.

Key statutes include the Communications Act 2003, the Broadcasting Act 1990, the Broadcasting Act 1996, the Office of Communications Act 2002, the Copyright, Designs and Patents Act 1988, and some provisions of the Telecommunications Act 1984.

*Related topic(s): AGENCY; CONTRACT LAW; COPYRIGHT; CRIMINAL LAW; DATA PROTECTION; FREEDOM of INFORMATION; INFORMATION TECHNOLOGY LAW; INTELLECTUAL PROPERTY LAW; TELECOMMUNICATIONS LAW.*

| Author(s) | Title | Edition | Publisher | Year |
|---|---|---|---|---|
| Robertson, Geoffrey and Nicol, Andrew | *Robertson & Nicol on Media Law* [S,P,A] | 6th | Sweet & Maxwell | 2016 |
| Arnold, Richard | *Performers' Rights* [P,A] | 5th | Sweet & Maxwell | 2015 |
| Price, Monroe E. and Verhulst, Stefaan, eds. | *Routledge Handbook of Media Law* [P] | | Routledge | 2015 |
| Fosbrook, Deborah and Laing, Adrian C. | *Media and Business Contracts Handbook* [P] | 5th | Sweet & Maxwell | 2014 |
| Gibbons, Thomas | *Media Law in the United Kingdom* [P,A] | 2nd | Wolters Kluwer | 2014 |
| Owen, Lynette, ed. | *Clark's Publishing Agreements: A Book of Precedents* [P] | 9th | Bloomsbury Professional | 2013 |
| Jones, Hugh and Benson, Christopher | *Publishing Law* [S,N] | 4th | Routledge | 2011 |
| Carey, Peter, *et al.* | *Media Law* [S,N] | 5th | Sweet & Maxwell | 2010 |

| Author(s) | Title | Edition | Publisher | Year |
|---|---|---|---|---|
| Crown, Giles, Bray, Oliver, and Earle, Rupert | *Advertising Law and Regulation* [P] | 2nd | Bloomsbury Professional | 2010 |
| Goldberg, David, Sutter, Gavin, and Walden, Ian | *Media Law and Practice* [P] | | Oxford University Press | 2009 |
| Kanaar, Nick and Phillips, Chris | *Bagehot & Kanaar on Music Business Agreements* [P] | 3rd | Sweet & Maxwell | 2009 |
| Harrison, Ann | *Music: The Business—The Essential Guide to the Law and the Deals* [P,N] | 6th | Virgin Books | 2014 |
| Verow, Richard, Kanaar, Nicholas, and Overs, Estelle | *Entertainment Law Handbook* [P] | | The Law Society | 2007 |

## Noteworthy websites, blogs, etc.:

### BLOGS

- City University, Centre for Law, Justice, and Journalism Blog (https://blogs.city.ac.uk/cljj/)
- International Forum for Responsible Media (Inforrm), Blog (https://inforrm.wordpress.com/about/)
- Paul Howcroft, Art Law London (http://artlawlondon.blogspot.co.uk)

# MEDICAL LAW

These titles deal with a wide range of topics related to the provision of health services. Subjects dealt with include the National Health Service, standards of services, negligence, medical ethics, nursing, pharmacology, ophthalmology, dentistry, among others. Alternative health care practices such as chiropractic, naturopathy, osteopathy, and homeopathy would also fall under this heading.

Relevant statutes include the Care Standards Act 2000, Health Act 2006, Health and Social Care (Community Health and Standards) Act 2003, and the National Health Service Act 2006. There are also statutes specific to each of the various branches of medical service.

*Related topic(s): NEGLIGENCE; PROFESSIONAL CONDUCT and ETHICS; PROFESSIONAL NEGLIGENCE; SOCIAL SECURITY and WELFARE LAW; TORT LAW.*

| **Author(s)** | **Title** | **Edition** | **Publisher** | **Year** |
|---|---|---|---|---|
| Mardell, Julie and Serfozo, Kate | *Personal Injury and Clinical Negligence Litigation* [S,P] | | College of Law Publishing | Annual |
| Grubb, Andrew, Laing, Judith, and McHale, Jean | *Principles of Medical Law* [P,A] | 4th | Oxford University Press | 2016* |
| Jones, Michael | *Medical Negligence* [P,A] | 5th | Sweet & Maxwell | 2016 |
| Begley, Laura and Aldous, Grahame, eds. | *Clinical Negligence Claims: A Practical Guide* [P] | 3rd | 9 Gough Square | 2015 |
| Dimond, Bridgit | *Legal Aspects of Nursing* [S,N] | 7th | Pearson Education | 2015 |
| Powers, Michael, Barton, Anthony, and Jackson, Barry | *Clinical Negligence* [P,A] | 5th | Bloomsbury Professional | 2015 |
| Pattinson, Shaun | *Medical Law and Ethics* [S] | 4th | Sweet & Maxwell | 2014 |
| Appelbe, Gordon E., and Wingfield, Joy | *Dale and Appelbe's Pharmacy and Medicines Law* [S,P] | 10th | Pharmaceutical Press | 2013 |
| Foster, Charles | *Medical Law: A Very Short Introduction* [S,A] | | Oxford University Press | 2013 |
| Jackson, Emily | *Medical Law: Text, Cases, and Materials* [S] | 3rd | Oxford University Press | 2013 |
| Mason, J.K., | *Mason & McCall Smith's* | 9th | Oxford University | 2013 |

| Author(s) | Title | Edition | Publisher | Year |
|---|---|---|---|---|
| Laurie, G.T., and Aziz, M. | *Law and Medical Ethics* [S] | | Press | |
| Glynn, Joanna and Gomez, David | *The Regulation of Healthcare Professionals: Law, Principle and Process* [P] | | Sweet & Maxwell | 2012 |
| Herring, Jonathan | *Medical Law* [S] | | Oxford University Press | 2011 |
| Foster, Charles, ed. | *Medical Law: Precedents for Lawyers* [P] | | Wildy, Simmonds & Hill | 2010 |
| McHale, Jean | *Health Care Law: Text and Materials* [S] | 2nd | Sweet & Maxwell | 2006 |

## Noteworthy websites, blogs, etc.:

### WEBSITES

- Medical Negligence, (http://www.medneg.com/)

# MENTAL HEALTH LAW

This topic involves a variety of legal issues related to mental health and capacity including the provision of mental health services, the powers and responsibilities of mental health tribunals, the responsibility of others for the legal and financial affairs and property of mental health patients, and the legal effects of their incapacity.

The principal statutes in this area are the Mental Capacity Act 2005 and the Mental Health Act 1983 the former dealing primarily with managing the affairs of those with mental incapacity and latter dealing with the provision of treatment to those suffering a mental disorder as well as the guardianship of such individuals. Other relevant enactments are the Human Rights Act 1998 and the European Convention on Human Rights.

For mental incapacity in relation to criminal matters, see CRIMINAL LAW.

*Related topic(s): ADMINISTRATIVE LAW; AGENCY; CRIMINAL LAW; HOUSING LAW; HUMAN RIGHTS and CIVIL LIBERTIES; MEDICAL LAW; POLICE and PUBLIC ORDER LAW; SOCIAL SECURITY and WELFARE LAW.*

| Author(s) | Title | Edition | Publisher | Year |
|---|---|---|---|---|
| Hale, Brenda | *Mental Health Law* [P] | 6th | Sweet & Maxwell | 2016 |
| Johnston, Christopher | *Medical Treatment Decisions and the Law: The Mental Capacity Act in Action* [P] | 3rd | Bloomsbury Professional | 2016 |
| Ashton, Gordon, ed. | *Court of Protection Practice 2015* [P] | | Jordan Publishing | 2015* |
| Ashton, Gordon, ed. | *Mental Capacity: Law and Practice* [P] | 3rd | Jordan Publishing | 2015 |
| Jones, Richard | *Mental Health Act Manual* [P] | 18th | Sweet & Maxwell | 2015* |
| Butler, Michael | *A Practitioner's Guide to Mental Health Law* [P] | | Wildy, Simmonds & Hill | 2014 |
| Jones, Richard | *Mental Capacity Act Manual* [P] | 6th | Sweet & Maxwell | 2014 |
| Bartlet Peter and Sandland, Ralph | *Mental Health Law: Policy and Practice* [P,A] | 4th | Oxford University Press | 2013 |
| Butler, Jonathan | *Mental Health Tribunals: Law, Practice, and Procedure* [P] | 2nd | Jordan Publishing | 2013 |

| Author(s) | Title | Edition | Publisher | Year |
|---|---|---|---|---|
| Fennell, Philip | Mental Health: Law and Practice [P] | 2nd | Jordan Publishing | 2011 |
| Mahendra, Dr. Bala | *Family Psychiatric Practice: A Guide for Lawyers* [P] | | Jordan Publishing | 2010 |
| Gostin, Lawrence, *et al.* | *Principles of Mental Health Law and Policy* [P,A] | | Oxford University Press | 2010 |
| Terrell, Martin | *A Practitioner's Guide to the Court of Protection* [P] | 3rd | Bloomsbury Professional | 2009 |
| Bartlett, Peter | *Blackstone's Guide to the Mental Capacity Act 2005* [P] | 2nd | Oxford University Press | 2008 |
| Greaney, Nicola, Morris, Fennella, and Taylor, Beverley | *Mental Capacity: A Guide to the New Law* [P] | 2nd | The Law Society | 2008 |
| Weereratne, Aswini, *et al.* | *The Mental Capacity Act 2005* [P] | | LexisNexis Butterworths | 2008 |

## Noteworthy websites, blogs, etc.:

### WEBSITE

- Mental Health Law Online (http://www.mentalhealthlaw.co.uk/Main_Page)

# MILITARY LAW

Military law is the term employed to the law in relation to the country's land, naval, and air forces including all reserve units thereunder. Most titles deal with one of two distinct research streams: the legal underpinnings of the forces themselves or the law as it relates to disciplinary proceedings against military personnel.

The legal foundations of the land and air forces are essentially statutory whereas those of the naval forces have evolved from the royal prerogative. In regard to the land and air forces there are a multitude of statutes and statutory instruments. Some leading ones are the Armed Forces Acts (of which there are numerous iterations, recent ones being 1991, 1996, and 2001), the Army Act 1955 and 1992, Reserve Forces Act 1980, the Air Force Act 1955, and the Courts-Martial (Appeals) Act 1951 and 1968. As there is no statutory authority for the Royal Navy there is no Act similar to the Air Force and Army Acts however there is the Naval Discipline Act 1957. Military procurement is dealt with by the Defence Reform Act 2014.

*Related topic(s): CONSTITUTIONAL LAW; CRIMINAL LAW; CROWN LAW; INTERNATIONAL CRIMINAL LAW; INTERNATIONAL LAW; PRACTICE & PROCEDURE (CIVIL).*

| Author(s) | Title | Edition | Publisher | Year |
|---|---|---|---|---|
| | *The Queen's Regulations for the Army* [P] | | The Stationery Office | LL |
| | *The Queen's Regulations for the Royal Air Force* [P] | | The Stationery Office | LL |
| Bano, Andrew | *War Pensions and Armed Forces Compensation: Law and Practice* [P] | | Wildy, Simmonds & Hill | 2016 |
| Gill, Terry and Fleck, Dieter, eds. | *The Handbook of the International Law of Military Operations* [P,A] | 2nd | Oxford University Press | 2015 |
| Head, Michael | *Domestic Deployment of the Armed Forces: Military Powers, Law, and Human Rights* [A] | | Ashgate | 2009 |
| Whetham, David | *Ethics, Law, and Military Operations* [A] | | Palgrave Macmillan | 2010 |
| Blackett, His Honourable Judge Jeff | *Rant on The Court Martial and Service Law* [P] | 3rd | Oxford University Press | 2009 |

| Author(s) | Title | Edition | Publisher | Year |
|---|---|---|---|---|
| Boothby, William H. | *Weapons and the Law of Armed Conflict* [A] | 2nd | Oxford University Press | 2016 |
| UK Ministry of Defence | *The Manual of the Law of Armed Conflict* [P,A] | | Oxford University Press | 2005 |

# NEGLIGENCE

Negligence is a specific tort (and constitutes a sizable portion of all tort law) under which one can be found liable for actions or omissions which result in harm or financial damage to another. This is a longstanding, fundamental area of the common law and as such is ruled by very little statutory authority.

There are in essence three requirements of a successful negligence action: a demonstrated duty of care was owed the plaintiff by the defendant; a proven breach of the standard of care by the defendant occurred; and that harm to the plaintiff resulted from said breach of the standard of care.

Much writing on this topic deals with defining duty and standard of care and proving causation. Other sub-topics include defences to a negligence suit (such as plaintiff's assumption of risk), contributory negligence, and remedies in a negligence action, which is normally payment of damages.

Two related areas of tort law are occupier's liability (the liability of a property owner for injury caused on his premises) and products liability which is when harm occurs from a negligently manufactured or defective product. In relation to the former there are two statutes of note: the Occupier's Liability Act 1957 and the Occupier's Liability Act 1984. For products liability, see CONSUMER LAW.

*Related topic(s): CONSUMER LAW; PROFESSIONAL NEGLIGENCE; TORT LAW.*

| Author(s) | Title | Edition | Publisher | Year |
|---|---|---|---|---|
| Jones, Michael | *Medical Negligence* [P,A] | 5th | Sweet & Maxwell | 2016 |
| Aldous, Grahame, ed. | *Clinical Negligence Claims: A Practical Guide* [P] | 3rd | 9 Gough Square | 2015 |
| Powers, Michael, Harris, Nigel, and Barton, Anthony | *Clinical Negligence* [P,A] | 5th | Bloomsbury Professional | 2015 |
| Green, Sarah | *Causation in Negligence* [A,S] | | Hart | 2014 |
| Walton, Christopher, *et al.*, eds. | *Charlesworth & Percy on Negligence* [P,A] | 13th | Sweet & Maxwell | 2014* |
| Buckley, Richard A. | *The Law of Negligence and Nuisance* [P,A] | 5th | LexisNexis Butterworths | 2011 |
| Maddison, His Honour Judge David, *et al.* | *Bingham's Negligence Cases* [P] | 5th | Sweet & Maxwell | 2002 |

## Noteworthy websites, blogs, etc.:

### WEBSITES

- Carruthers Law (firm), (http://www.carruthers-law.co.uk/news-articles/#.Vs8iyZwrK71)

# NUISANCE

Nuisance, a specific tort, is the heading of law under which a person can sue another if the enjoyment or use of their property has in some way been affected by the activities (or omissions) of the other. It is a particularly long standing area of the common law to which there are few applicable statutes.

There are private and public nuisances, the latter of which applies to activities which affect an entire class of persons and there are common law and statutory nuisances, i.e., one which is created by a particular statutory provision. There is also criminal nuisance which usually arises from a statutory nuisance (e.g., the Environmental Protection Act 1990) but can also arise from a common law nuisance.

An important case in this area of law is that of *Fletcher v. Rylands and Horrocks* (1866) LR 1 Exch 26, which was a case, originally framed in trespass, which had a profound effect on the development of this topic in that it created a context under which strict liability could be found in nuisance. It has come to be known as the Rule in *Rylands v. Fletcher*.

The most common types of nuisance involve pollution or contamination of air, water, and/or ground and other activities affecting quiet use and enjoyment and use of one's property, such as noise. Certain anti-social behaviours are viewed as nuisance and as such the Anti-Social Behaviour Act 2003 has some relevant provisions.

Most works dealing with nuisance will also touch upon the defences available in a nuisance action as well as remedies, which are normally injunction or damages.

*Related topic(s): AGRICULTURE LAW; ANIMAL LAW; CONSTRUCTION LAW; CRIMINAL LAW; ENERGY & NATURAL RESOURCES LAW; ENVIRONMENTAL LAW; POLICE and PUBLIC ORDER LAW; PROPERTY LAW; REAL PROPERTY; TORT LAW.*

| **Author(s)** | **Title** | **Edition** | **Publisher** | **Year** |
|---|---|---|---|---|
| Beever, Allan | *The Law of Private Nuisance* [A] | | Hart Publishing | 2013 |
| Buckley, Richard | *The Law of Negligence and Nuisance* [P,A] | 5th | LexisNexis Butterworths | 2011 |
| Malcolm, Rosalind and Pointing, John | *Statutory Nuisance: Law and Practice* [P] | 2nd | Oxford University Press | 2011 |
| Murphy, John | *Law of Nuisance* [P,A] | | Oxford University Press | 2010 |

| Author(s) | Title | Edition | Publisher | Year |
|---|---|---|---|---|
| McCracken, Robert, Jones, Gregory, and Pereira, James | Statutory Nuisance: Law and Practice [P] | 3rd | Bloomsbury Professional | 2008 |
| Elvin, David and Karas, Jonathan | *Unlawful Interference with Land: Nuisance, Trespass, Covenants and Statutes* [P,A] | 2nd | Sweet & Maxwell | 2002 |
| Hughes, David | *Air Pollution: Law and Regulation* [P] | | Jordan Publishing | 1998 |

# PARTNERSHIP LAW

A partnership is a particular type of commercial relationship in which two or more persons engage in business with the aim of making a profit. These partners are often referred to as a 'firm'. A partner is not normally subject to limited liability unless the partnership was established as a limited partnership pursuant to the Limited Partnership Act 1907 or as a limited liability partnership in accord with the Limited Liability Partnerships Act 2000. Limited partners may not take part in the management of the firm and for this reason a firm cannot be comprised solely of limited partners and there needs to be some general partners. A limited liability partnership is a corporate entity with a legal personality separate from that of its members.

There are only a few key statutes important to this topic: the Partnership Act 1890, the Limited Partnership Act 1907, and the Limited Liability Partnership Act 2000. Some provisions of the Companies Act 2006 are also instructive.

*Related topic(s): COMMERCIAL LAW; COMPANY LAW; CONTRACT LAW.*

| Author(s) | Title | Edition | Publisher | Year |
|---|---|---|---|---|
| I'Anson Banks, Roderick, ed. | *Encyclopedia of Professional Partnerships* [P] | | Sweet & Maxwell | LL |
| Callman, Jeremy, Berry, Elspeth, and Moule, Jos. | *The Law of Partnerships and LLPs: A Practical Guide* [P] | | Jordan | 2016 |
| Whittaker, John and Machell, John | *The Law of Limited Liability Partnerships* [P] | 4th | Bloomsbury Professional | 2016 |
| Blackett-Ord, Mark and Haren, Sarah | *Partnership Law* [P] | 5th | Bloomsbury Professional | 2015 |
| Morse, Geoffrey | *Partnership Law* [S] | 8th | Oxford University Press | 2015 |
| Smith, Paula | *Limited Liability Partnerships Handbook* [P] | 3rd | Bloomsbury Professional | 2012 |
| Morse, Geoffrey, *et al.* | *Palmer's Limited Liability Partnership Law* [P] | 2nd | Sweet & Maxwell | 2011 |
| Berry, Elspeth | *Partnership and LLP Law* [P] | | Wildy, Simmonds & Hill | 2010 |
| I'Anson Banks, Roderick | *Lindley & Banks on Partnership* [P,A] | 19th | Sweet & Maxwell | 2010* |

| Author(s) | Title | Edition | Publisher | Year |
|---|---|---|---|---|
| Machell, John, Haywood, Jennifer, and Mather, James, eds. | *LLP Legislation Handbook* [P] | | Bloomsbury Professional | 2010 |

# PATENTS

A patent is essentially a state-granted monopoly for production of some kind of functional device or formula. These grants date back to the reign of Elizabeth I and until the 1970s were granted by the Sovereign. Since the Patents Act 1977 came into force they have been granted under the authority of that Act.

Important matters include the application process, duration of the patent (currently twenty years), the ownership and assignability of a patent, the administration of the Patent Office, among others.

A patent is an example of intellectual property and is also dealt with in titles listed under that heading.

Relevant statutes are the Patents Act 1977, Patents Act 2004, and Copyright, Designs, and Patents Act 1988.

*Related topic(s): DESIGNS; INTELLECTUAL PROPERTY.*

| Author(s) | Title | Edition | Publisher | Year |
|---|---|---|---|---|
| Anderson, Mark | *Drafting Patent and Know-How Licence Agreements* [P] | | Oxford University Press | 2016 |
| Birss, His Honour Judge Colin, *et al.* | *Terrell on the Law of Patents* [P,A] | 18th | Sweet & Maxwell | 2016 |
| Cole, Paul G. and Jones, Stephen F., eds. | *CIPA Guide to the Patents Acts* [P] | 8th | Sweet & Maxwell | 2015 |
| Cook, Trevor | *A User's Guide to Patents* [P] | 4th | Bloomsbury Professional | 2015 |
| Roughton, Ashley, Johnson, Phillip, and Cook, Trevor | *The Modern Law of Patents* [P] | 3rd | LexisNexis Butterworths | 2014 |
| Visser, Derk | *The Annotated European Patent Convention 2000* [P] | 22nd | H. Tel | 2014 |
| Cornish, William R. and Llewelyn, David | *Intellectual Property: Patents, Copyright, Trade Marks, and Allied Rights* [S,P,A] | 8th | Sweet & Maxwell | 2013 |
| Jacob, The Rt. Hon. Sir Robin, Alexander, Daniel, and Fisher, Matthew | *A Guidebook to Intellectual Property: Patents, Trade Marks, Copyright and Designs* [S] | 6th | Hart Publishing | 2013 |

| Author(s) | Title | Edition | Publisher | Year |
|---|---|---|---|---|
| Fox, Nicholas | *A Guide to the EPC 2000: A Practitioner's Guide to the Law* [P] | | Chartered Institute of Patent Agents | 2010 |
| Pila, Justine | *The Requirement for an Invention in Patent Law* [P,A] | | Oxford University Press | 2010 |
| Fisher, Matthew | *Fundamentals of Patent Law: Interpretation and Scope of Protection* [P,A] | | Hart Publishing | 2007 |

## Noteworthy websites, blogs, etc.:

### BLOGS

- Mark Anderson, IP Draughts (https://ipdraughts.wordpress.com/)
- Fieldfisher (firm), Intellectual Property Blog (http://intellectualpropertyblog.fieldfisher.com/)
- LexisNexis, World of IP and IT (WIPIT) Blog (http://blogs.lexisnexis.co.uk/wipit/)
- Shireen Smith, Azrights News and Media (www.venables.co.uk/blogs.htm)
- Neil J. Wilkof, et al., The IPKat (www.ipkat.com)

# PENSIONS LAW

These titles deal with the complex and multifaceted subject of the law of pensions. There are, in essence, five different types of pension schemes extant in the United Kingdom: state retirement pensions (see also SOCIAL SECURITY and WELFARE LAW); occupational pension schemes; public service pensions; retirement annuity contracts; and personal pensions.

In order to protect the rights of employees, future and current pensioners, pensions are heavily regulated with an attempt to balance the needs of employees/ pensioners and those of employers and pension funds themselves. Relevant statutes include the Pensions Act 1995, the Pensions Act 2004, and the Pension Schemes Act 1993 among other statutes and many statutory instruments.

*Related topic(s): ADMINISTRATIVE LAW; EMPLOYMENT AND LABOUR LAW; TAXATION.*

| Author(s) | Title | Edition | Publisher | Year |
|---|---|---|---|---|
| | *Tolley's Pensions Law* [P] | | LexisNexis Butterworths | LL |
| | *Law of Pension Schemes* [P] | | Sweet & Maxwell | LL |
| Ellison, Robin, ed. | *Pensions Law and Practice with Precedents* [P] | | Sweet & Maxwell | LL |
| Ure, Alec, ed. | *Butterworths Pension Legislation Service* [P] | | LexisNexis Butterworths | LL |
| Bano, Andrew | *War Pensions and Armed Forces Compensation: Law and Practice* [P] | | Wildy, Simmonds & Hill | 2016 |
| Pollard, David | *Employment Law and Pensions* [P,N] | | Bloomsbury Professional | 2016 |
| Nabarro Pensions Team | *Pensions Law Handbook* [P] | 12th | Bloomsbury Professional | 2015 |
| Pollard, David | *The Law of Pension Trusts* [P,A] | | Oxford University Press | 2013 |
| Ellison, Robin | *The Pension Trustee's Handbook* [N] | 7th | Thorogood | 2012 |
| Weir, Clive | *Pensions for Family Lawyers: A Resolution Guide* [P] | | Resolution (Solicitors Family Law Association) | 2010 |

| Author(s) | Title | Edition | Publisher | Year |
|---|---|---|---|---|
| Derbyshire, Wyn and Hardy, Stephen | *Pensions and Employment Law: Issues at the Interface* [P] | | Sweet & Maxwell | 2008 |
| Ure, Alec and Moffat, Gavin | *Tolley's Guide to The Pensions Act 2004: A Complete Update of the Law and Practice* [P] | | LexisNexis Butterworths | 2006 |
| Jenkins, Martin and Poore, Martin | *Blackstone's Guide to The Pensions Act 2004* [P] | | Oxford University Press | 2005 |
| Marshall, Jane, McKenna, Catherine, and Graham, Elizabeth | *Pensions Act 2004: A Guide to the New Law* [P] | | The Law Society | 2005 |

## Noteworthy websites, blogs, etc.:

### WEBSITE

- LexisNexis, Lexis Web: Pensions (http://lexisweb.co.uk/groups/pensions/default.aspx)

### BLOG

- Allen Overy (firm), Pensions Talk (http://www.pensionstalk.co.uk/)

# PERSONAL INJURY LAW

Personal injury law is a particularly active area of tort law in which plaintiffs seek damages from alleged tortfeasors for actions or omissions which have caused them physical and/or mental injury. Many of the titles deal specifically with the matter of calculating damages, both pecuniary (to replace lost income) and non-pecuniary (primarily for pain and suffering).

As this is a subset of tort law there is little authoritative legislation but there is a wealth of instructive jurisprudence.

*Related topic(s): LIMITATION; NEGLIGENCE; TORT LAW; REMEDIES, DAMAGES, and RESTITUTION.*

| Author(s) | Title | Edition | Publisher | Year |
|---|---|---|---|---|
| De Haas, Margaret, Q.C. and Goldrein, Iain S., Q.C. | *Butterworths Personal Injury Litigation Service* [P] | | LexisNexis Butterworths | LL |
| Marshall, David and McCarthy, Frances | *Association of Personal Injury Lawyers (APIL) Personal Injury Law, Practice, and Precedents* [P] | | Jordan Publishing | LL |
| Norris, William, Cory-Wright, Charles, and Andrews, Peter | *Kemp & Kemp: Quantum of Damages* [P] | | Sweet & Maxwell | LL |
| Ritchie, Andrew, ed. | *Personal Injury Law, Practice and Procedure* [P] | | Sweet & Maxwell | LL |
| Mardell, Julie and Serfozo, Kate | *Personal Injury and Clinical Negligence Litigation 2016* [S,P] | | College of Law Publishing | Annual |
| Foster, Charles and Bradley, Ben | *APIL Guide to Tripping and Slipping Cases* [P] | 2nd | Jordan Publishing | 2015 |
| Buchan, Andrew, Kennedy, Jenny, and Woolf, Eliot | *Personal Injury Practice* [P] | 6th | Bloomsbury Professional | 2014 |
| Curran, Patrick | *Personal Injury Pleadings* [P] | 5th | Sweet & Maxwell | 2014 |
| North, Sir Peter | *Occupier's Liability* [A,P] | 2nd | Oxford University Press | 2014 |

| Author(s) | Title | Edition | Publisher | Year |
|---|---|---|---|---|
| Exall, Gordon | *Munkman on Damages for Personal Injuries and Death* [P] | 12th | LexisNexis Butterworths | 2011 |
| Exall, Gordon | *Personal Injury Litigation* [P] | | Wildy, Simmonds & Hill | 2011 |
| Pether, Michael, *et al.* | *Bingham & Berryman's Personal Injury and Motor Claims Cases* [P] | 13th | LexisNexis Butterworths | 2010* |
| Burton, Frank, *et al.*, eds. | *PIBA Personal Injury Handbook* [P] | 3rd | Jordan Publishing | 2007 |
| Kevan, Tim, *et al.* | *Fraudulent and Exaggerated Claims in Personal Injury* [P] | | XPL Law | 2006 |
| Waller, Nicholas | *Personal Injury Handbook* [P] | | The Law Society | 2005 |

## Noteworthy websites, blogs, etc.:

### WEBSITE

- LexisNexis, Lexis Web: Personal Injury (http://lexisweb.co.uk/groups/personal-injury/default.aspx)

### BLOGS

- Fieldfisher (firm), Serious Injury Blog (http://www.fieldfisher.com/personalinjury/blog/)
- Peter Kirk, Personal Injury Blog (https://kirkonpersonalinjury.wordpress.com/pi-blog/)
- Law Brief Publishing, PI Brief Update (http://www.pibriefblog.com/)
- Nigel Poole, Learned Friend (http://nigelpooleqc.blogspot.co.uk/)
- John Spencer, UK Personal Injury Solicitor (http://john-spencer.blogspot.co.uk/)

# PLANNING LAW

Planning law deals with the rules and requirements which surround the development of land in the United Kingdom. It is driven by specific statutes, primarily the Town and Country Planning Act 1990, the Planning Act 2008, the Local Government, Planning and Land Act 1980, and the Planning (Listed Buildings and Conservation Areas) Act 1990 and by a multitude of statutory instruments, most of which have been promulgated under authority of the Town and Country Planning Act 1990.

Planning is both national and local in scope in that some plans are national and others are developed by local authorities. An important sub-topic is that of acquisition and appropriation of land by the Crown and the appropriate compensation therefor.

*Related topic(s): ADMINISTRATIVE LAW; AGRICULTURE LAW; CONSTRUCTION LAW; CROWN LAW; ENVIRONMENTAL LAW; LOCAL GOVERNMENT LAW; REAL PROPERTY; TAXATION.*

| Author(s) | Title | Edition | Publisher | Year |
|---|---|---|---|---|
| Grant, Malcolm | *Encyclopedia of Planning Law and Practice* [P] | | Sweet & Maxwell | LL |
| Little, A.J. | *Planning Controls and their Enforcement* [P] | 8th | Shaw & Sons | LL |
| Tromans, Stephen and Turrall-Clarke, Robert | *Planning Law, Practice, & Precedents* [P] | | Sweet & Maxwell | LL |
| Blackhall, J. Cameron and Willmore, Chris | *Planning Law and Practice* [S,P] | 4th | Routledge-Cavendish | 2016 |
| Travers, David, Q.C., Grant, Edward, and Lambert, Emmaline | *Planning Enforcement* [P] | | Wildy, Simmonds & Hill | 2015 |
| Moore, Victor | *A Practical Approach to Planning Law* [S,P] | 13th | Oxford University Press | 2014 |
| Duxbury, Robert | *Telling & Duxbury's Planning Law and Procedure* [S,P] | 15th | Oxford University Press | 2012 |
| Roots, Guy, Q.C., *et al.* | *The Law of Compulsory Purchase* [P] | 2nd | Bloomsbury Professional | 2011 |

| Author(s) | Title | Edition | Publisher | Year |
|---|---|---|---|---|
| Cullingworth, Barry and Nadin, Vincent | *Town and Country Planning in the UK* [S] | 14th | Routledge | 2006 |

## Noteworthy websites, blogs, etc.:

### BLOGS

- LexisNexis, Purpose Built Blog (http://blogs.lexisnexis.co.uk/purposebuilt/)
- Mills & Reeve (firm), Plan-It Law (http://www.plan-it-law.com/)

# POLICE and PUBLIC ORDER

Titles under this heading deal with one or the other of police or public order. Police law is that which deals with the powers and duties of modern police forces. The keeping of the sovereign's peace has been the responsibility of constables since the 1600s. The common law of constables has evolved into the current statutory law related to policing. Its basic statutes included the Police Act 1996 and the Police Act 1997, the Police Reform Act 2002, and the Police and Criminal Evidence Act 1984. A major change in the administration of policing came about with the Police Reform and Social Responsibility Act 2011 which put police forces under the control of elected Police and Crime Commissioners.

Most works dealing with police law will touch upon such matters as the administration of the police service, training standards, conduct of police and complaints related thereto.

Public order is a particular subset of criminal law which deals with such activities as riot, public disturbance, affray, harassment, incitement to racial or religious hatred, public alcohol consumption, certain types of nuisance (e.g., noise, exposure to profanity, among others), and squatting.

*Related topic(s): ADMINISTRATIVE LAW; CONSTITUTIONAL LAW; CRIMINAL LAW; HUMAN RIGHTS and CIVIL LIBERTIES; MILITARY LAW; NUISANCE.*

| Author(s) | Title | Edition | Publisher | Year |
|---|---|---|---|---|
| Beggs, John and Davies, Hugh | *Police Misconduct, Complaints, and Public Regulation* [P] | 2nd | Oxford University Press | 2016 |
| Cook, Tony and Tattersall, Andrew | *Blackstone's Senior Investigating Officer's Handbook* [N] | 4th | Oxford University Press | 2016 |
| Smart, Huw | *Blackstone's Custody Officer's Manual* [N] | 6th | Oxford University Press | 2016 |
| Conner, Paul, *et al.* | *Blackstone's Police Manuals 2016* [4 vols.] [N] | | Oxford University Press | 2015* |
| Edwards, Andrew and Hardcastle, Matthew | *Blackstone's Police Station Handbook* [N,P] | | Oxford University Press | 2015 |
| English, Jack and Card, Richard | *Police Law* [P,N] | 14th | Oxford University Press | 2015 |

| Author(s) | Title | Edition | Publisher | Year |
|---|---|---|---|---|
| Harfield, Clive, Bridges, Ian, and Sampson, Fraser, eds. | *Blackstone's Police Operational Handbook 2015* 2 vols (1: Law; 2: Practice and Procedure) [N] | | Oxford University Press | 2015* |
| Ozin, Paul, Norton, Heather, and Spivey, Perry | *PACE: A Practical Guide to the Police and Criminal Evidence Act 1984* [N,P] | 4th | Oxford University Press | 2015 |
| Zander, Michael, Q.C. | *The Police and Criminal Evidence Act 1984* [P] 🖱 | 7th | Sweet & Maxwell | 2015 |
| Stone, Richard | *The Law of Entry, Search & Seizure* [P,N] 🖱 | 5th | Oxford University Press | 2013 |
| Beggs, John, Street, Amy, and Thomas, George, eds. | *Public Order: Law and Practice* [P] 🖱 | | Oxford University Press | 2012 |
| Thornton, His Honour Judge Peter, Q.C., *et al.* | *The Law of Public Order and Protest* [P,A] | | Oxford University Press | 2010 |
| Jason-Lloyd, Leonard | *An Introduction to Policing and Police Powers* [S,N] | 2nd | Routledge-Cavendish | 2005 |

## Noteworthy websites, blogs, etc.:

### WEBSITE

- The Home Office, Publications re PACE [Police & Criminal Evidence Act] (https://www.gov.uk/government/publications)

### BLOG

- Iain Gould, Actions Against the Police Solicitor: The Blog of a Police Misconduct Claims Lawyer (iaingould.co.uk)

# PRACTICE and PROCEDURE (CIVIL)

Civil procedure is the procedural (as opposed to the substantive) law in effect in all legal actions other than in criminal matters. It rests on a number of foundations both statutory and jurisprudential. The main statutory underpinnings can be found in enactments such as the Civil Procedure Act 1997, the Senior Courts Act 1981, the County Courts Act 1984, and the Tribunals, Courts, and Enforcement Act 2007. These statutes establish the objectives of civil procedure rules, but the rules themselves are found almost exclusively in the Civil Procedure Rules 1998 (CPR) and the multitude of Practice Directives which supplements the CPR.

These rules deal with every step of the process of litigating a particular matter in British courts. There are rules dealing with: procedures prior to the commencement of actions; the commencement of actions; how parties are to be served; who may be party to an action; the particulars of specific types of actions, e.g., injunctions; disclosure of documents and evidence; the trial process itself; and the enforcement of judgements, among numerous others.

*Related topic(s): ADMINISTRATIVE LAW; ARBITRATION and DISPUTE RESOLUTION; CONSTITUTIONAL LAW; DRAFTING and LEGAL WRITING; ENGLISH LEGAL SYSTEM; LEGAL SKILLS and METHOD; REMEDIES, DAMAGES, and RESTITUTION.*

| Author(s) | Title | Edition | Publisher | Year |
|---|---|---|---|---|
| Thompson, P.K.J. and di Mambro, Louise, eds. | *LexisNexis Butterworths Civil Court Precedents* [P] | | LexisNexis Butterworths | LL |
| Turner, Robert, ed. | *Atkin's Court Forms* [P] | | LexisNexis Butterworths | LL |
| Jackson, the Rt. Hon. Lord Justice, ed. | *The White Book Service: Civil Procedure* [2 vols.] [P] | | Sweet & Maxwell | Annual |
| Kay, The Rt Hon Sir Maurice, Sime, Stuart, and French, Derek | *Blackstone's Civil Practice 2016* [P] | | Oxford University Press | Annual |
| Laws, the Rt. Hon. Lord Justice, *et al.* | *Civil Court Service (The Brown Book)* [P] | | Jordan Publishing | Annual |
| Thompson, P.K.J. and di Mambro, Louise | *The Civil Court Practice: The Green Book* [2 vols.] [P] | | LexisNexis Butterworths | Annual |

| Author(s) | Title | Edition | Publisher | Year |
|---|---|---|---|---|
| Bean, David, Parry, Isabel, and Burns, Andrew | *Injunctions* [P] | 12th | Sweet & Maxwell | 2015 |
| Blair, The Rt. Hon. Mr. Justice, *et al.*, eds. | *Bullen & Leake & Jacob's Precedents of Pleadings* [P] | 18th | Sweet & Maxwell | 2015* |
| Briggs, Adrian | *Civil Jurisdiction and Judgments* [P,A] | 6th | Informa | 2015 |
| O'Hare, John and Browne, Kevin | *O'Hare & Browne: Civil Litigation* [P,S] | 17th | Sweet & Maxwell | 2015 |
| Sime, Stuart | *A Practical Approach to Civil Procedure* [S,P] | 18th | Oxford University Press | 2015 |
| Jacobs, Edward | *Tribunal Practice and Procedure: Tribunals under the Tribunals, Courts, and Enforcement Act 2007* [P] | 3rd | Legal Action Group | 2014 |
| Leabeater, James, *et al.* | *Civil Appeals: Principle and Procedure* [P,A] 🖱 | 2nd | Sweet & Maxwell | 2014 |
| Hurst, Peter | *Civil Costs* [P] 🖱 | 5th | Sweet & Maxwell | 2013 |
| Zuckerman, Adrian | *Zuckerman on Civil Procedure: Principles and Practice* [P] | 3rd | Sweet & Maxwell | 2013 |
| Bowers, John and Misra, Eleena | *Procedure in Civil Courts and Tribunals* [P] | 3rd | Wildy, Simmonds & Hill | 2010 |
| Sandbrook, Claire | *Enforcement of a Judgment* [P] | 11th | Sweet & Maxwell | 2010 |
| Handley, The Hon. Mr. Justice Kenneth R. and Spencer Bower, George | *Spencer Bower and Handley: Res Judicata* [P] | 4th | LexisNexis Butterworths | 2009 |
| Supperstone, Michael and Knapman, Lynn, eds. | *Administrative Court Practice* [P] | 2nd | Oxford University Press | 2008 |
| Lang, Beverley, *et al.*, eds. | *Administrative Court: Practice and Procedure* [P] | | Sweet & Maxwell | 2006 |

## Noteworthy websites, blogs, etc.:

### WEBSITE

- Carruthers Law (firm), (http://www.carruthers-law.co.uk/news-articles/#.Vs8iyZwrK71)

**BLOG**

- Chris Dale, eDisclosure Information Project (https://chrisdale.wordpress.com/)

# PRACTICE and PROCEDURE (CRIMINAL)

Just as the titles in the above topic deal with the procedural rules surrounding a civil action, those below deal with the guiding rules of prosecuting a criminal action. Similar to those of civil procedure, the sources of these rules are mostly statutory augmented by a wealth of interpretive and instructive case law.

There are fundamental statutes in effect including the Police and Criminal Evidence Act 1984 (PACE), the Criminal Procedure and Investigation Act 1996, the Magistrates' Court Act 1980, and the Criminal Justice Act 2003, among others. The major source of rules, however, is the voluminous Criminal Procedure Rules 2005 (CrimPR) which are supplemented by a number of Practice Directions. A very instructive source are the PACE Codes of Practice which apply primarily to pre-trial processes such as arrest, detention, and questioning.

*Related topic(s): CONSTITUTIONAL LAW; CRIMINAL LAW; ENGLISH LEGAL SYSTEM; HUMAN RIGHTS and CIVIL LIBERTIES; INTERNATIONAL CRMINAL LAW; POLICE and PUBLIC ORDER LAW; PRISON LAW; REMEDIES, DAMAGES, and RESTTUTION.*

| Author(s) | Title | Edition | Publisher | Year |
|---|---|---|---|---|
| Ormerod, David, ed. | *Blackstone's Criminal Practice 2016* [P] | | Oxford University Press | Annual |
| Richardson, James, ed. | *Archbold: Criminal Pleading, Evidence and Practice* [P] | | Sweet & Maxwell | Annual |
| Barnes, Barbara, ed. | *Archbold Magistrates Courts Criminal Practice* [P] | | Sweet & Maxwell | Annual |
| Carr, Paul and Turner, Adrian, eds. | *Butterworths Stone's Justices' Manual 2016* [3 vols.] [P] | | LexisNexis Butterworths | Annual |
| Jones, Daniel, Stewart, Greg, and Bennathan, Joel, Q.C. | *Criminal Appeals Handbook* [P] | | Bloomsbury Professional | 2015 |
| Sprack, John | *A Practical Approach to Criminal Procedure* [S,P] | 15th | Oxford University Press | 2015 |
| Roveri, Alessandro | *Magistrates' Court Criminal Practice 2014* [P] | | Jordans | 2014 |

| Author(s) | Title | Edition | Publisher | Year |
|---|---|---|---|---|
| Young, David, Summers, Mark, and Corker, David | Abuse of Process in Criminal Proceedings [P] | 4th | Bloomsbury Professional | 2014 |
| Rahman, Pakeeza and Rendell, Tony | *Youth Court Guide* [P] | 5th | Bloomsbury Professional | 2012 |
| Taylor, Paul, ed. | *Taylor on Criminal Appeals* [P] | 2nd | Oxford University Press | 2012 |
| Ashworth, Andrew and Redmayne, Michael | *The Criminal Process* [S] | 4th | Oxford University Press | 2010 |
| Corker, David and Parkinson, Stephen | *Disclosure in Criminal Proceedings* [P] | | Oxford University Press | 2009 |
| Handley, The Hon. Mr. Justice Kenneth R. and Spencer Bower, George | *Spencer Bower and Handley: Res Judicata* [P,A] | 4th | LexisNexis Butterworths | 2009 |
| Keogh, Andrew | *Criminal Procedure Rules: A Guide to Key Changes* [P] | 2nd | The Law Society | 2008 |

## Noteworthy websites, blogs, etc.:

### WEBSITES

- Criminal Law & Justice Weekly (http://www.criminallawandjustice.co.uk/)
- Crown Prosecution Service (CPS), Legal Guidance (http://www.cps.gov.uk/legal/)
- The Home Office, Publications re PACE [Police & Criminal Evidence Act] (https://www.gov.uk/government/publications)
- LexisNexis, Lexis Web: Crime (http://lexisweb.co.uk/groups/crime/default.aspx)

### BLOG

- Dan Bunting, Lyndon Harris, and Sara Williams, UK Criminal Law Blog (http://ukcriminallawblog.com/category/current-awareness/caselaw-update/)

# PRISON LAW

This topic deals with the law in regard to the creation, administration, and governance of prisons and the treatment of prisoners. At its core are the provisions of the Prison Act 1952 (which applies exclusively to England and Wales) authorising the Secretary of State for Justice to make rules for the management of Her Majesty's prisons.

*Related topic(s): ADMINISTRATIVE LAW; CRIMINAL LAW; DISCRIMINATION LAW; HUMAN RIGHTS and CIVIL LIBERTIES; INTERNATIONAL CRIMINAL LAW; MENTAL HEALTH LAW; POLICE and PUBLIC ORDER LAW; PRACTICE & PROCEDURE (CRIMINAL).*

| Author(s) | Title | Edition | Publisher | Year |
|---|---|---|---|---|
| Livingstone, Stephen, Owen Tim, Q.C., Macdonald, Alison | *Livingstone, Owen, and Macdonald on Prison Law* [P,A] | 5th | Oxford University Press | 2015 |
| Arnott, Hamish and Creighton, Simon | *Parole Board Hearings: Law and Practice* [P] | 3rd | Legal Action Group | 2013 |
| Obi, Margaret | *Blackstone's Prison Law Handbook 2014-2015* [P] | | Oxford University Press | 2013 |
| Easton, Susan | *Prisoners' Rights: Principles and Practice* [A] | | Routledge | 2011 |
| Creighton, Simon and Arnott, Hamish | *Prisoners: Law and Practice* [P] | | Legal Action Group | 2009 |
| Obi, Margaret | *Prison Law: A Practical Guide* [P] | | The Law Society | 2008 |

# PRIVACY LAW

Also known as 'confidence' this relatively new and expanding area of the law deals with the rights of individuals to keep certain information about themselves confidential and obligates data gathering entities to respect that confidentiality. There are numerous contexts in which privacy law is at issue, but the four principal ones are: health information, employment, financial data, and with regard to information gathered by public authorities.

It is an area grounded mostly in the common law with only one directly applicable statute, the Access to Health Records Act 1990, and Article 7 of the Charter of Fundamental Rights of the European Union, which includes the right to private life as a fundamental right. Privacy law's proper place in the common law is the subject of some conjecture with some asserting its correct place is in tort law, others arguing it is a property law matter, and still others seeing any remedies as being equitable.

*Related topic(s): BANKING and FINANCE LAW; CONSUMER LAW; DATA PROTECTION; EMPLOYMENT AND LABOUR LAW; FREEDOM of INFORMATION; HUMAN RIGHTS and CIVIL LIBERTIES; INTELLECTUAL PROPERTY LAW; LIBEL and SLANDER.*

| Author(s) | Title | Edition | Publisher | Year |
|---|---|---|---|---|
| Jay, Rosemary, Boardman, Ruth, and Grant, Hazel | *Encyclopedia of Data Protection and Privacy* [P] | | Sweet & Maxwell | LL |
| Warby, Mark and Moreham, Nicole, eds. | *Tugendhat and Christie: The Law of Privacy and the Media* [P,A] | 3rd | Oxford University Press | 2016 |
| Richardson, Janice | *Law and the Philosophy of Privacy* [A] | | Routledge | 2015 |
| Wacks, Raymond | *Privacy: A Very Short Introduction* [S] | 2nd | Oxford University Press | 2015 |
| Coppel, Philip | *Information Rights: Law and Practice* [P,A] | 4th | Hart Publishing | 2014 |
| Goldrein, Iain, Q.C. | *Privacy Injunctions and the Media: A Practice Manual* [P] | | Hart Publishing | 2012 |
| Doley, Cameron, and Mullis, Alistair, eds. | *Carter-Ruck on Libel and Privacy* [P,A] | 6th | LexisNexis Butterworths | 2010 |

| Author(s) | Title | Edition | Publisher | Year |
|---|---|---|---|---|
| Mathieson, Keith, ed. | *Privacy Law Handbook* [P] | | The Law Society | 2010 |
| Clayton, Richard and Tomlinson, Hugh | *The Law of Human Rights: Privacy and Freedom of Expression* [P,A] | 2nd | Oxford University Press | 2010 |
| Deacon, Robert, Lipton, Nigel, and Pinker, Robert | *Privacy and Personality Rights: Commercial Exploitation and Protection* [P] | | Jordan Publishing | 2010 |
| Moore, Dudley | *Privacy and the Press* [P,A] | 2nd | XPL Law | 2006 |
| Cooper, Jonathan | *Privacy* [P,A] | | Sweet & Maxwell | 2005 |

## Noteworthy websites, blogs, etc.:

### BLOGS

- Amberhawk Associates, Hawktalk (http://amberhawk.typepad.com/amberhawk/)
- Fieldfisher (firm), Privacy and Information Law Blog (http://privacylawblog.fieldfisher.com/)
- Information Commissioner's Office, ICO Blog (https://iconewsblog.wordpress.com/)
- International Forum for Responsible Media (Inforrm), Blog (https://inforrm.wordpress.com/about/)
- Olswang (firm), Datonomy: The Data Protection Blog (http://datonomy.eu/)
- Timothy Pitt-Payne, Anya Proops, Robin Hopkins, and Christopher Knight, Panopticon (http://panopticonblog.com/)
- RPC (firm), RPC Data and Privacy Law (http://www.rpc.co.uk/index.php?option=com_easyblog&view=latest&Itemid=107)
- Graham Smith, Cyberleagle (http://cyberleagle.blogspot.co.uk/)

# PROFESSIONAL CONDUCT and ETHICS

While there are numerous professions in England, many of which are self-regulating, such as actuaries, architects, engineers, and surveyors, among others, the great majority of titles in this topic deal with norms of professional ethics and conduct on the part of solicitors and barristers. In spite of the perception by a great many people, the legal profession is one to which ethical conduct is fundamental and as such is a subject of great interest and importance.

There is also a large of body of work related to ethics and medicine and its associated disciplines, such as pharmacy. For such titles, see MEDICAL LAW.

*Related topic(s): ACCOUNTING LAW; CONSTRUCTION LAW; LEGAL PRACTICE MANAGEMENT; MEDICAL LAW; PROFESSIONAL NEGLIGENCE.*

| Author(s) | Title | Edition | Publisher | Year |
|---|---|---|---|---|
| Bacon, Nicholas and Garrod, Simon | *The Bar Handbook* [P] | | LexisNexis Butterworths | Annual |
| Hopper, Andrew and Treverton-Jones, Gregory | *The Solicitors' Handbook* [P] | | The Law Society | Annual |
| Camp, Peter | *Solicitors and the Accounts Rule: A Compliance Handbook* [P] | 4th | The Law Society | 2016 |
| Pattenden, Rosemary | *The Law of Professional-Client Confidentiality* [P,A] | 2nd | Oxford University Press | 2016 |
| Boon, Andrew | *Lawyers' Ethics and Professional Responsibility* [P] | | Bloomsbury | 2015 |
| Gould, John, ed. | *Law of Legal Services* | | Jordan Publishing | 2015 |
| Treverton-Jones, Q.C., Gregory, Foster, Alison, Q.C., and Hanif, Saima | *Disciplinary and Regulatory Proceedings* [P] | 8th | Jordan Publishing | 2015 |
| Boon, Andrew | *The Ethics and Conduct of Lawyers in the United Kingdom* [S] | 3rd | Hart Publishing | 2014 |
| McPeake, Robert, ed. | *Bar Manual: Professional Ethics* [S,P] | 16th | Oxford University Press | 2014 |

| Author(s) | Title | Edition | Publisher | Year |
|---|---|---|---|---|
| Toulson, R.G. and Phipps, C.M. | *Confidentiality* [P] | 3rd | Sweet & Maxwell | 2012 |
| Hirst, Christina | *Ethics and Professional Conduct for Chartered Surveyors* [N] | 2nd | Royal Institute of Chartered Surveyors | 2011 |
| Hollander, Charles and Salzedo, Simon | *Conflicts of Interest* [P] | | Sweet & Maxwell | 2011 |
| Billins, Roger | *Solicitors' Duties and Liabilities* [P] | 2nd | The Law Society | 2009 |

# PROFESSIONAL NEGLIGENCE

These works deal with the law of negligence in the specific context of the liability of members of recognized professions. The core concepts of negligence, namely duty of care, standard of care, and harm resulting from their breach, apply but when it comes to professionals the duty of care is more obvious and the standard expected is demonstrably higher than that demanded of non-professionals. Most of these works deal with negligence on the part of legal professionals but many others deal with medical negligence as well. Other professions are not as well-represented in this literature.

*Related topic(s): CONSTRUCTION LAW; CONSUMER LAW; CONTRACT LAW; LEGAL SKILLS and METHOD; LIMITATION; MEDICAL LAW; NEGLIGENCE; PRACTICE & PROCEDURE (CIVIL); PROFESSONAL CONDUCT and ETHICS; REMEDIES, DAMAGES, and RESTITUTION; TORT LAW.*

| Author(s) | Title | Edition | Publisher | Year |
|---|---|---|---|---|
| Simpson, Mark, ed. | *Professional Negligence and Liability* [P] | | Sweet & Maxwell | LL |
| Mardell, Julie and Serfozo, Kate | *Personal Injury and Clinical Negligence Litigation* [S,P] | | College of Law Publishing | Annual |
| Treverton-Jones, Gregory, Q.C., Foster, Alison, Q.C., and Hanif, Saima | *Disciplinary and Regulatory Proceedings* [P] | 8th | Jordan Publishing | 2015 |
| Davies, Mark | *The Law of Professional Immunities* [A] | | Oxford University Press | 2014 |
| Flenley, William and Leech, Thomas | *Solicitor's Negligence* [P,A] | 3rd | Bloomsbury Professional | 2012 |
| Powell, John, Stewart, Roger, and Jackson, The Rt. Hon. Mr. Justice | *Jackson & Powell on Professional Liability* [P,A] | 7th | Sweet & Maxwell | 2011* |
| Mulheron, Rachael | *Medical Negligence: Non-Patient and Third Party Claims* [P] | | Ashgate | 2010 |

| Author(s) | Title | Edition | Publisher | Year |
|---|---|---|---|---|
| Speaight, Anthony and Stone, Gregory | *Architects' Legal Handbook: The Law for Architects* [N] | 9th | Architectural Press | 2010 |
| Murdoch, John | *Law of Estate Agency* [N,P] | 5th | Estates Gazette | 2009 |
| Davies, Mark | *Solicitors' Negligence and Liability* [P,A] | | Oxford University Press | 2008 |
| Murdoch, John | *Negligence in Valuations and Surveys: Case in Point* [P,N] | 2nd | Royal Institute of Chartered Surveyors | 2008 |
| Patten, Ben | *Professional Negligence in Construction* [P,A] | | Taylor & Francis | 2003 |

## Noteworthy websites, blogs, etc.:

### WEBSITE

- Carruthers Law (firm), (http://www.carruthers-law.co.uk/news-articles/#.Vs8iyZwrK71)

### BLOG

- piCalculator (software) and 1 Chancery Lane (Barristers chambers), pnBLAWG—the professional negligence blog (http://www.pnblawg.co.uk/)

# PROPERTY LAW

This ancient and complex area of the common law relates to the ownership of "things". The titles here are general in scope and deal mostly with law as it relates to chattels or "movables" as opposed to "immovables" such as land. It also excludes ownership of ideas. For titles related to property in land, see REAL PROPERTY; for those dealing with property in ideas, see INTELLECTUAL PROPERTY; COPYRIGHT; DESIGNS; and/or PATENTS.

The law of property is one to which few legislative enactments apply directly although some sections of the Law of Property Act 1925 touch upon some general issues.

There are numerous subtopics within this subject including, amongst many others, bailment (the entrusting of property to another for safekeeping), the law of finders, and property related torts such as trover (recovery of damages for the wrongful taking of property), and detinue (recovery for the wrongful detention of goods). The law of pledge and pawn is another area of interest.

*Related topic(s): ANIMAL LAW; CONTRACT LAW; COPYRIGHT; EQUITY & TRUSTS; FAMILY LAW; INTELLECTUAL PROPERTY LAW; PATENTS; SALE of GOODS; SHIPPING, TRANSPORT, and MARITIME LAW; TORT LAW; WILLS and PROBATE.*

| Author(s) | Title | Edition | Publisher | Year |
|---|---|---|---|---|
| Davies, Margaret | *Property* [S,A] | | Routledge | 2015 |
| Smith, Roger J. | *Property Law* [S] | 8th | Pearson Higher Education | 2014 |
| Davey, Jonathan and Faulkner, Benjamin, eds. | *Butterworths Property Law Handbook* [P] | 10th | LexisNexis Butterworths | 2013* |
| Palmer, Norman | *Palmer on Bailment* [P,A] | 3rd | Sweet & Maxwell | 2009 |
| Stanyer, Ann | *Personal Chattels: Law, Practice, and Tax—with Precedents* [P] | | Sweet & Maxwell | 2009 |
| McFarlane, Ben | *The Structure of Property Law* [S] | | Hart Publishing | 2008 |
| Clarke, Alison and Kohler, Paul | *Property Law: Commentary and Materials* [S] | | Cambridge University Press | 2005 |

## REAL PROPERTY LAW

Also known as 'land law' the law of real property is ancient with some its concepts having their origin in pre-Norman Conquest Anglo-Saxon law. It is established firmly in the common law, but there is an overlay of statutory provisions as well, such as the Land Registration Act 2002, the Law of Property Act 1925, and the Settled Land Act 1925.

Real property law is complex with a myriad of subtopics and side issues frequently in play. These include the types of possession, freehold (fee simple) and leasehold, possession and title, registration of title, equitable rights in land, effects of co-ownership, joint tenancies and tenancies-in-common, trespass, adverse possession, easements and rights of entry, conveyancing and sale of land, and covenants.

*Related topic(s): AGRICULTURE LAW; CONTRACT LAW; CROWN LAW; ENERGY and NATURAL RESOURCES LAW; FAMILY LAW; HOUSING LAW; INSURANCE LAW; LANDLORD and TENANT LAW; LOANS and MORTGAGES; NUISANCE; PLANNING LAW; PROPERTY LAW; TAXATION.*

| Author(s) | Title | Edition | Publisher | Year |
|---|---|---|---|---|
| Bickford-Smith, Stephen, Redler, Alistair, and Smith, Andrew | *Party Walls: Law and Practice* [P] | 4th | Jordan Publishing | 2016 |
| Dixon, Martin | *Modern Land Law* [S] | 10th | Routledge | 2016 |
| Sara, Colin | *Boundaries and Easements* [P] | 6th | Sweet & Maxwell | 2015 |
| Mackenzie, Judith-Anne and Phillips, Mary | *Textbook on Land Law* [S] | 15th | Oxford University Press | 2014 |
| Rainey, Philip, *et al.*, eds. | *Megarry's Manual of the Law of Real Property* [P] | 9th | Sweet & Maxwell | 2014 |
| Stevens, John and Pearce, Robert | *Land Law* [S,P] | 5th | Sweet & Maxwell | 2013 |
| Stroud, April | *Making Sense of Land Law* [S] | 4th | Palgrave Macmillan | 2013 |
| Gaunt, Jonathan and Morgan, The Rt. Hon. Mr. Justice | *Gale on Easements* [P] | 19th | Sweet & Maxwell | 2012 |

| Author(s) | Title | Edition | Publisher | Year |
|---|---|---|---|---|
| Harpum, Charles, Bridge, Stuart, and Dixon, Martin | Megarry & Wade: The Law of Real Property [S,P,A] | 8th | Sweet & Maxwell | 2012 |
| Thompson, Mark P. | *Modern Land Law* [S] | 5th | Oxford University Press | 2012 |
| Agnew, Donald and Morris, Amanda | *Neighbour Disputes: A Guide to the Law and Practice* [P] | 2nd | Wildy, Simmonds & Hill | 2011 |
| Gray, Kevin and Gray, Susan Francis | *Land Law* [S] | 7th | Oxford University Press | 2011 |
| Jourdan, Stephen, Q.C. and Radley-Gardner, Oliver | *Adverse Possession* [P,A] | 2nd | Bloomsbury Professional | 2011 |
| Boothroyd, Jan E. | *Garner's Local Land Charges* [P] | 14th | Sweet & Maxwell | 2010 |
| Gravells, Nigel P. | *Land Law: Text and Materials* | 4th | Sweet & Maxwell | 2010 |
| Aldridge, Hon. Trevor, Q.C. | *Boundaries, Walls, and Fences* [P] | 10th | Sweet & Maxwell | 2009 |
| Burn, E.H. and Cartwright, John | *Maudsley & Burn's Land Law: Cases and Materials* [S] | 9th | Oxford University Press | 2009 |
| Pugh-Smith, John, Sinclair, Graham, and Upton, William | *Neighbours and the Law* [P] | 5th | Sweet & Maxwell | 2009 |

## Noteworthy websites, blogs, etc.:

### WEBSITES

- The Law Society, Property—Residential (http://www.lawsociety.org.uk/practice-areas/property-residential/)
- LexisNexis, Lexis Web: Property (http://lexisweb.co.uk/groups/property/default.aspx)
- John Maynard Boundaries Ltd., The Boundary Problems Website (http://www.boundary-problems.co.uk/boundary-problems/frontpage.html)
- PracticalConveyancing.co.uk (http://www.practicalconveyancing.co.uk/)
- Gary Webber, The Property Law Website (http://www.propertylawuk.net/)

## BLOGS

- Clutton Cox (firm), Conveyancing blog (http://www.cluttoncox.co.uk/site/blog/conveyancingblog/)
- Clutton Cox (firm), Estate agency blog (http://www.cluttoncox.co.uk/site/blog/estateagencyblog/)
- Her Majesty's Land Registry, Land Registry Blog (http://blog.landregistry.gov.uk/)
- LexisNexis, Purpose Built Blog (http://blogs.lexisnexis.co.uk/purposebuilt/)

## REMEDIES, DAMAGES, and RESTITUTION

This broad category covers the various possible awards for a successful civil action: remedies, such as injunction, which proscribes a particular activity to be undertaken by a defendant, or specific performance which mandates a particular act be performed; damages, the reward of payment as recompense for a wrong done to the plaintiff; or restitution, which is essentially repayment for a defendant's unjust enrichment.

The law of damages is longstanding and grows out of the common law of tort, contract, equity, and to a lesser extent, property. Its major principles deal with assessing and measuring damages. The law of restitution was originally seen as a subset of contract law but a landmark 1991 House of Lords case, *Lipkin Gorman (a firm) v. Karpnale* [1991] 3 WLR 10, [1991] 2 AC 548 established it as a recognizable area of law independent of contract.

This topic is largely grounded in case law, but there are some statutes to note: the Damages Act 1996, the County Courts Act 1984, the Senior Courts Act 1981, the Civil Liability (Contribution) Act 1978, and the Law Reform (Frustrated Contracts) Act 1943.

*Related topic(s): COMMERCIAL LAW; CONSUMER LAW; CONTRACT LAW; FRAUD and MISPREPESENTATION; LIMITATION; NEGLIGENCE; NUISANCE; PERSONAL INJURY LAW; PRACTICE & PROCEDURE (CIVIL); PROFESSIONAL NEGLIGENCE; SALE of GOODS; TORT LAW.*

| Author(s) | Title | Edition | Publisher | Year |
|---|---|---|---|---|
| Burrows, Andrew | *Remedies for Tort and Breach of Contract* [S,A,P] | 4th | Oxford University Press | 2016 |
| Virgo, Graham | *The Principles of the Law of Restitution* [A,P] | 3rd | Oxford University Press | 2016 |
| Bean, David, Parry, Isabel, and Burns, Andrew | *Injunctions* [P] | 12th | Sweet & Maxwell | 2015 |
| McFarlane, Ben and Mitchell, Charles | *Hayton & Mitchell: Texts, Cases and Materials on the Law of Trusts and Equitable Remedies* [P] | 14th | Sweet & Maxwell | 2015 |
| Rose, Francis, ed. | *Blackstone's Statutes on Contracts, Tort & Restitution 2015-16* [P,S] | | Oxford University Press | 2015* |

| Author(s) | Title | Edition | Publisher | Year |
|---|---|---|---|---|
| Kramer, Adam | *The Law of Contract Damages* [P,A] | | Hart | 2014 |
| Lewis, Clive | *Judicial Remedies in Public Law* [P,A] | 5th | Sweet & Maxwell | 2014 |
| McGregor, Harvey | *McGregor on Damages* [P,A] | 19th | Sweet & Maxwell | 2014 |
| Allen, Simon, Bowley, Ivan, and Davies, Hugh | *APIL Guide to Damages* [P] | 3rd | Jordan Publishing | 2013 |
| Mitchell, Charles, Mitchell, Paul, and Watterson, Stephen | *Goff & Jones: The Law of Unjust Enrichment* [A,P] | 8th | Sweet & Maxwell | 2011 |
| Burrows, Andrew | *The Law of Restitution* [S,A,P] | 3rd | Oxford University Press | 2010 |
| Tettenborn, Andrew | *The Law of Damages* [P,A] | 2nd | LexisNexis Butterworths | 2010 |
| Burrows, Andrew, McKendrick, Ewan, and Edelman, James | *Cases and Materials on the Law of Restitution* [S] | 2nd | Oxford University Press | 2006 |
| Goff, Lord of Chieveley and Jones, Gareth | *Goff & Jones: The Law of Restitution* [A,P] | 7th | Sweet & Maxwell | 2006 |
| Zakrzewski, Rafal | *Remedies Reclassified* [A] | | Oxford University Press | 2005 |
| Rotherham, Craig, *et al.* | *The Law of Restitution* [P,A] | | LexisNexis Butterworths | 2003 |

## Noteworthy websites, blogs, etc.:

### WEBSITE

- Stewart Dunn, The Law of Damages (http://www.stewartdunn.com/)

# RESIDENTIAL TENANCIES LAW

Normally treated under Landlord & Tenant Law this listing deals with titles which provide information on that topic in the context of residential properties whereas 'Landlord and Tenant' in this book deals primarily with commercial, non-residential tenancies. The titles below deal with the nature of residential tenancy relationships and the rights and obligations of residential tenants and landlords.

There are essentially three types of residential tenancies: Rent Act tenancies (entered into prior to 1989) which provide secure tenancies; assured tenancies, which provide some security of tenancy but give the landlord more leeway in charging market rate-based rents and make it easier to evict tenants who fail to pay rent; and assured shorthold tenancies, which are normally of six months duration.

There is an important human rights component to residential tenancies law in that tenancies may not be refused for discriminatory reasons.

Residential tenancy is a subject with many longstanding common law principles but there is also a lot of relevant legislation such as numerous Housing Acts, the most recent from 2004, (and those of 1985 and 1988 being the most vigorous); various Landlord and Tenant Acts (among which those of 1954 and 1987 are the most germane); the Leasehold Reform Act 1967; the Leasehold Reform, Housing, and Urban Development Act 1993; the Protection from Eviction Act 1977; and the Rent Act 1977.

*Related topic(s): DISCRIMINATION LAW; HOUSING LAW; HUMAN RIGHTS and CIVIL LIBERTIES; LANDLORD and TENANT LAW; PROPERTY LAW; REAL PROPERTY.*

| Author(s) | Title | Edition | Publisher | Year |
|---|---|---|---|---|
| Aldridge, Trevor M. | *Leasehold Law* [P] | | Sweet & Maxwell | LL |
| Arden, Andrew and Partington, Martin | *Housing Law* [P] | | Sweet & Maxwell | LL |
| Driscoll, James, Williams, Del, and Boston, Charles | *Handbook of Residential Tenancies* [P] | | Sweet & Maxwell | LL |
| Reynolds, Kirk, Q.C., Featherstonehaugh, Guy, and Bernstein, Ronald | *Handbook of Rent Review* [P] | | Sweet & Maxwell | LL |
| Garner, Simon and Frith, Alexandra | *A Practical Approach to Landlord and Tenant* [S,P] | 7th | Oxford University Press | 2013 |

| Author(s) | Title | Edition | Publisher | Year |
|---|---|---|---|---|
| Roche, Helen, ed. | *Residential Property Practice: An Expert Guide* [P] | | Ark Group | 2013 |
| Webber, Gary and Dovar, Daniel | *Residential Possession Proceedings* [P] | 9th | Sweet & Maxwell | 2013 |
| Driscoll, James | *LexisNexis Butterworths Residential Landlord and Tenant Handbook* [P] | 6th | LexisNexis Butterworths | 2012 |
| Colbey, Richard and O'Brien, Niamh | *Residential Tenancies* [P] | 5th | Wildy, Simmonds & Hill | 2009 |
| Ward, Charles | *Residential Leaseholders Handbook* [N] | | Estates Gazette | 2006 |

## Noteworthy websites, blogs, etc.:

### BLOGS

- Clutton Cox (firm), Landlord and tenant blog (http://www.cluttoncox.co.uk/site/blog/landlordandtenantblog/)
- PainSmith Solicitors, PainSmith Landlord and Tenant blog (https://blog.painsmith.co.uk/)
- Tessa Shepperson, The Landlord Law Blog (http://www.landlordlawblog.co.uk/)
- The Landlord Law BLOG Case Reports (http://www.landlordlawblog.co.uk/category/law-case-report/)

# ROAD TRAFFIC LAW

In the 1950s the government of Harold Macmillan made a transport policy decision to provide more support to the development of the highway network in Britain at the expense of railway expansion leading eventually to the development of the motorway system and the upgrade of many secondary highways. The result has been that Britain has become a country small in size but with a huge number of motor vehicles operating on its often congested roads. As such a very important area of law is that of road traffic. This is a huge, almost entirely statute-driven, area of law which includes such subtopics as the rules of the road, vehicle requirements, the licensing of drivers and vehicles, insurance requirements, rules with regard to public passenger and goods vehicles, the hauling of hazardous materials, and offences and penalties for breaches of road traffic law.

The principal statutes in this subject are: The Road Traffic Act 1988, the Road Traffic Offenders Act 1988, the Road Safety Act 2006, the Public Passenger Vehicles Act 1981, the Road Traffic Regulation Act 1984, and various Transport Acts (1968, 1980, 1982, 1985, and 2000). Local authorities are also empowered to make road traffic rules to be used on their roads.

*Related topic(s): CRIMINAL LAW; HEALTH and SAFETY; INSURANCE LAW; LOCAL GOVERNMENT LAW; NEGLIGENCE; PERSONAL INJURY LAW; PLANNING LAW; SHIPPING, TRANSPORT, and MARITIME LAW; TAXATION; TORT LAW.*

| **Author(s)** | **Title** | **Edition** | **Publisher** | **Year** |
|---|---|---|---|---|
| Sauvain, Stephen | *Encyclopedia of Highway Law and Practice* [P,N] | | Sweet & Maxwell | LL |
| Ward, Robert | *Encyclopedia of Road Traffic Law and Practice* [P,N] | | Sweet & Maxwell | LL |
| Button, James T.H. | *Button on Taxis: Licensing Law and Practice* [P,N] | 4th | Bloomsbury Professional | 2016 |
| Callow, Pauline M. | *Drink and Drug Case Notes* [P] | 3rd | Wildy, Simmonds & Hill | 2015 |
| McCormac, Kevin, *et al.*, eds. | *Wilkinson's Road Traffic Offences* [P] | 27th | Sweet & Maxwell | 2015* |
| Cooper, Simon and Orme, Michael | *Road Traffic Law* [N,S] | 2nd | Oxford University Press | 2009 |
| Callow, Pauline M. | *The Drink-Drive Offences: A Handbook for Practitioners* [P] | | Wildy, Simmonds & Hill | 2011 |

| Author(s) | Title | Edition | Publisher | Year |
|---|---|---|---|---|
| Carr, Kenneth, Lockhart, Frank, and Musters, Patrick | *Road Traffic Offences Handbook* [P] | | The Law Society | 2008 |
| Cunningham, Sally | *Driving Offences: Law, Policy, and Practice* [A] | | Ashgate | 2008 |
| Black, Jonathan | *Drinking and Driving Offences: Law and Practice* [P] | 2nd | The Law Society | 2006 |

## Noteworthy websites, blogs, etc.:

### WEBSITE

- Department for Transport (https://www.gov.uk/government/organisations/department-for-transport)

### BLOGS

- DWF (firm), The Lorry Lawyer (http://www.thelorrylawyer.com/blog/)
- Rothera Dawson Solicitors, Keep Me on the Road (http://www.keepmeontheroad.co.uk/blog/)

# SALE of GOODS

Sale of goods (and most services) as a legal subject is very much a subset of contract law. It applies to the sale of chattels which excludes money, negotiable instruments, and land, and is limited to sale rather exchange or barter. Many of its sub-issues are similar to that of general contract law: the formation, performance, effect, and breach of the contract of sale. Other issues specific to this topic include the rights of unpaid sellers, consumer protection, and international sale of goods.

This is a topic which, like contract law, is solidly grounded in case law, but there are some pertinent statutes, such as the Sale of Goods Act 1893 (which was essentially a codification of most of the existing common law provisions of the time), the Sale of Goods Act 1979, the Unfair Contract Terms Act 1977, and the Supply of Goods and Services Act 1982 (much of which deals with barter and exchange). An instructive statutory instrument is the Consumer Protection from Unfair Trading Regulations 2008.

*Related topic(s): COMMERCIAL LAW; CONSUMER LAW; CONTRACT LAW; DEBTOR & CREDITOR LAW; PROPERTY LAW.*

| Author(s) | Title | Edition | Publisher | Year |
|---|---|---|---|---|
| Bridge, Michael G., ed. | *Benjamin's Sale of Goods* [P,A] | 9th | Sweet & Maxwell | 2014* |
| Bridge, Michael | *The Sale of Goods* [P,A] | 3rd | Oxford University Press | 2014 |
| Christou, Richard | *Sale and Supply of Goods and Services* [P] | 3rd | Sweet & Maxwell | 2014 |
| Adams, John N. and MacQueen, Hector | *Atiyah's Sale of Goods* [S,P] | 12th | Pearson Higher Education | 2010 |
| Harvey, Brian W. and Meisel, Frank | *Auctions Law and Practice* [P] | 3rd | Oxford University Press | 2006 |
| McKendrick, Ewan | *Sale of Goods* [P,A] | | Informa | 2000 |

## SECURITIES

The term 'securities' is used to denote the many different financing devices available to companies such as shares (also called 'equities'), bonds, debentures, and derivatives, etc. The term comes from the fact that most of these, e.g., bonds and debentures, are secured and although shares are not they are often dealt with under this topic because they are a very common investment vehicle available to the public.

This topic blends centuries of common law development with recent legislation, the two most relevant enactments being the Financial Services and Markets Act 2000 and the Companies Act 2006.

Securities law deals with company shares (as does COMPANY LAW), classes of shares, their transfer, and the raising of share capital. It also touches upon securities regulation by the Financial Services Authority (FSA) and the rules related to the offering of securities to the public and the need for transparency in this process as mandated by the FSA Disclosure and Transparency Rules and the European Community's Transparency Obligations Directive 2004/109.

*Related topic(s): BANKING and FINANCE LAW; BILLS of EXCHANGE and LETTERS of CREDIT; COMPANY LAW; INTERNATIONAL INVESTMENT LAW; LOANS and MORTGAGES.*

| Author(s) | Title | Edition | Publisher | Year |
|---|---|---|---|---|
| Firth, Simon | *Derivatives: Law and Practice* [P] | | Sweet & Maxwell | LL |
| Sabalot, Deborah, ed. | *Butterworths Securities and Financial Services Law Handbook* [P] | | LexisNexis Butterworths | Annual |
| Astleford, Peter and Frase, Dick | *Hedge Funds and the Law* [P] | 2nd | Sweet & Maxwell | 2016 |
| Gabbert, Dale | *Hedge Funds* [P] | 2nd | LexisNexis Butterworths | 2016 |
| Ferran, Eilis and Ho, Look Chan | *Principles of Corporate Finance Law* [S] | 2nd | Oxford University Press | 2014 |
| Hudson, Alastair | *The Law of Finance* [P] | 2nd | Sweet & Maxwell | 2013 |
| Hudson, Alastair | *Securities Law* [P] | 2nd | Sweet & Maxwell | 2013 |
| Henderson, Schuyler K. | *Henderson on Derivatives* [P,A] | 2nd | LexisNexis Butterworths | 2010 |

| Author(s) | Title | Edition | Publisher | Year |
|---|---|---|---|---|
| Yates, Geoff and Hinchcliffe, Mike | *A Practical Guide to Private Equity Transactions* [P] | | Cambridge University Press | 2010 |
| Castagnino, John-Peter | *Derivatives: The Key Principles* [P] | 3rd | Oxford University Press | 2009 |
| Soundy, Mark, Spangler, Timothy, and Hampton, Alison | *A Practitioner's Guide to Private Equity* [P] | | City & Financial Publishing | 2009 |
| Cooke, Darryl J. | *Private Equity: Law and Practice* [P] | 5th | Sweet & Maxwell | 2008 |
| Moloney, Niamh | *EC Securities Regulation* [P,A] | 2nd | Oxford University Press | 2008 |
| Hudson, Alastair | *The Law on Financial Derivatives* [P,A] | 4th | Sweet & Maxwell | 2006 |

## SHIPPING, TRANSPORT, and MARITIME LAW

This topic deals with the carriage of goods (and sometimes passengers) by road, rail, sea, and air. It is one which is based in common law, legislation, and international convention. There is a degree of similarity between rail, road, and air carriage but shipping (carriage by sea) has elements which are distinct from the others.

Statutes to note are: the Carriage by Air Act 1961, the Carriage of Goods by Road Act 1965, the Carriage of Goods by Sea Act 1971, the Carriage of Goods by Sea Act 1992, the Merchant Shipping Act 1995, and the Railways and Transport Safety Act 2003. Important international conventions include the United Nations Convention on the Law of Sea 1982, the Convention Concerning International Carriage by Rail, the Convention on the Contract for the International Carriage of Goods by Road, and numerous iterations of the Convention for the Unification of Certain Rules for International Carriage by Air.

Most works dealing with carriage in general will touch upon such matters as the distinction between common and private carriers, contracts of carriage and bills of lading, charter parties, carriage of dangerous goods and animals, and defences and remedies available in relevant litigation. In the context of shipping by sea and in maritime law issues of interest include the ability of various courts to hear admiralty cases, pilotage and towing, security of the sea, and rights of salvage.

*Related topic(s): ANIMAL LAW; CONFLICT of LAWS; CONTRACT LAW; ENGLISH LEGAL SYSTEM; EUROPEAN UNION LAW; HEALTH and SAFETY; INSURANCE LAW; INTERNATIONAL TRADE LAW; PRACTICE & PROCEDURE (CIVIL); ROAD TRAFFIC LAW; TORT LAW.*

| Author(s) | Title | Edition | Publisher | Year |
|---|---|---|---|---|
| Derrington, Sarah C. and Turner, James M. | *The Law and Practice of Admiralty Matters* [P] | 2nd | Oxford University Press | 2016 |
| Gault, Simon, *et al.*, eds. | *Marsden and Gault on Collisions at Sea* [P] | 14th | Sweet & Maxwell | 2016 |
| Reeder, John | *Brice on Maritime Law of Salvage* [P] | 6th | Sweet & Maxwell | 2016 |
| Rose, Francis | *Admiralty Claims* [P] | | Sweet & Maxwell | 2016 |
| Baughen, Simon | *Shipping Law* [S] | 6th | Routledge-Cavendish | 2015 |
| Eder, Bernard, *et al.* | *Scrutton on Charterparties and Bills of Lading* [P] | 23rd | Sweet & Maxwell | 2015 |

| Author(s) | Title | Edition | Publisher | Year |
|---|---|---|---|---|
| Coghlin, Terence, *et al.* | *Time Charters* [P] | 7th | Informa | 2014 |
| Merkin, Robert | *Marine Insurance Legislation* [P] | 5th | Informa | 2014 |
| Bugden, Paul and Lamont-Black, Simonne | *Goods in Transit and Freight Forwarding* [P] | 3rd | Sweet & Maxwell | 2013 |
| Mandaraka-Sheppard, Aleka | *Modern Maritime Law* [P,S] | 3rd | Informa | 2013 |
| Tiberg, Hugo | *The Law of Demurrage* [P,A] | 5th | Sweet & Maxwell | 2013 |
| Treitel, Guenter H. and Reynolds, F.M.B. | *Carver on Bills of Lading* [P] | 3rd | Sweet & Maxwell | 2012 |
| Baatz, Yvonne, *et al.*, eds. | *Maritime Law* [P,S] | | Sweet & Maxwell | 2011 |
| Girvin, Stephen D. | *Carriage of Goods by Sea* [P] | 2nd | Oxford University Press | 2011 |
| Clarke, Malcolm | *Contracts of Carriage by Air* [P] | 2nd | Informa | 2010 |
| Harris, Brian | *Ridley's Law of the Carriage of Goods by Land, Sea, and Air* [S] | 8th | Sweet & Maxwell | 2010 |
| Thomas, D. Rhidian, ed. | *The Carriage of Goods by Sea under the Rotterdam Rules* [P] | | Informa | 2010 |
| Todd, Paul | *Maritime Fraud and Piracy* [P,A] | 2nd | Lloyd's List/Informa | 2010 |
| Wilson, John F. | *Carriage of Goods by Sea* [P] | 7th | Pearson Education | 2010 |
| Clarke, Malcolm | *Contracts of Carriage by Land and Air* [P] | 2nd | Informa | 2008 |

## Noteworthy websites, blogs, etc.:

### WEBSITES

- Department for Transport (https://www.gov.uk/government/organisations/department-for-transport
- Office of Rail and Road, Office of Rail Regulation (https://www.gov.uk/government/organisations/office-of-rail-regulation)
- Witherby Publishing Group, Seamanship International (http://www.seamanship.com/)

## BLOGS

- DWF (firm), The Lorry Lawyer (http://www.thelorrylawyer.com/blog/)
- Rothera Dawson Solicitors, Keep Me on the Road (http://www.keepmeontheroad.co.uk/blog/)

# SOCIAL SECURITY and WELFARE LAW

This is an enormous and complex area of law dealing with all branches of Britain's extensive social welfare system. Its administration falls within the purvew of the Secretary of State for Work and Pensions and has at its foundation numerous statutes including the Social Security Act 1998, the Social Security Contributions and Benefits Act 1992, the Social Security Administration Act 1992, the Jobseekers Act 1995, the Child Support, Pension and the Social Security Act 2000, and the Pensions Scheme Act 1993. As social security is an important human right there are European Union council regulations, particularly 1408/71 (on the application of social security schemes to employed persons and their families moving within the Community) and 574/72 (procedure for the implementation of 1408/71), and international conventions, as well as the domestic Human Rights Act 1998 which are also of fundamental importance. Significant changes to the breadth and depth of social benefits have recently been made by way of Welfare Reform Acts of 2007, 2009, and 2012.

Most titles in this area deal with the numerous social security and welfare programmes and benefits to which residents of the United Kingdom are entitled including income support, job-seekers' allowances, family allowance, national insurance (i.e., state pension and unemployment insurance), disability benefits, work-related injury compensation, housing benefit, war pension, maternity, child, and death benefits *inter alia*. Topics normally dealt with include the administration of the various programmes, the contributions scheme, and the process of entitlement decision-making and appeals therefrom.

*Related topic(s): ADMINISTRATIVE LAW; CHILDREN; DISCRIMINATION LAW; EUROPEAN UNION LAW; HOUSING LAW; HUMAN RIGHTS and CIVIL LIBERTIES; LOCAL GOVERNMENT LAW; PENSIONS LAW; RESIDENTIAL TENANCIES LAW.*

| Author(s) | Title | Edition | Publisher | Year |
|---|---|---|---|---|
| Jones, Richard, ed. | *Encyclopedia of Social Services and Child Care Law* [P] | | Sweet & Maxwell | LL |
| Bonner, David, *et al.* | *Social Security Legislation,* volumes I to IV [P] | | Sweet & Maxwell | Annual |
| Donegan, Barbara, *et al.*, eds. | *Welfare Benefits and Tax Credits Handbook 2015/2016* [P,N] | | Child Poverty Action Group | Annual |

| Author(s) | Title | Edition | Publisher | Year |
|---|---|---|---|---|
| Rowland, Mark and White, Robin | *Social Security Legislation Volume III—Administration, Adjudication, and the European Dimension 2016/2017* [P] | | Sweet & Maxwell | Annual |
| Wikeley, Nick, Williams, David, and Hooker, Ian | *Social Security Legislation Volume IV—Tax Credits and HMRC-Administered Social Security Benefits 2016/2017* [P] | | Sweet & Maxwell | Annual |
| Wood, Penny, *et al.* | *Social Security Legislation Volume II—Income Support, Jobseeker's Allowance, State Pension Credit, and the Social Fund 2016/2017* [P] | | Sweet & Maxwell | Annual |
| Bielanska, Caroline and Scolding, Fiona | *Health and Social Care Handbook* [P,N] | | Law Society Publishing | 2016 |
| Brammer, Alison | *Social Work Law* [N] | 4th | Pearson Education | 2015 |
| Butler, Jonathan | *Community Care Law and Local Authority Handbook* [P] | 3rd | Jordan Publishing | 2015 |
| Lister, Sam and Ward, Martin | *Guide to Housing Benefit and Council Tax Benefit 2014-17* [P,N] | | Chartered Institute of Housing | 2014 |
| Williams, John, Roberts, Gwyneth, and Griffiths, Aled | *Adult Social Care Law in England* [N] | | Palgrave Macmillan | 2014 |
| Clements, Luke and Thompson, Pauline, *et al.* | *Community Care and the Law* [P] | 5th | Legal Action Group | 2011 |
| Laird, Siobhan | *Practical Social Work Law: Analysing Court Cases and Inquiries* [N] | | Pearson Education | 2010 |
| Buck, Trevor | *The Social Fund: Law and Practice* [P] | 3rd | Sweet & Maxwell | 2009 |

## Noteworthy websites, blogs, etc.:

### WEBSITE

- Rightsnet (http://www.rightsnet.org.uk/)

# SPORTS LAW

There are only a few matters which can be solely categorised as 'sports law' but there are numerous aspects of other areas of law which come into play in the area of sports and games. The titles listed here deal with sports related elements of the following topics, all of which are dealt with elsewhere in this work: administrative law (e.g., the Football Licensing Authority), animal law (i.e., cruelty to animals), arbitration and dispute resolution (there are many dispute resolving mechanisms throughout amateur and professional sports), competition law (sports leagues often behave in ways which might be viewed as being in restraint of trade), contract law, criminal law (e.g., violent incidents during the course of play), intellectual property (particularly trade marks), local government law (public sporting events may only be conducted by way of a licence issued by the appropriate local authority) , and tort law (e.g., injured spectators).

Statutes of interest include the Cruelty to Animals Acts of 1835, 1849, and 1876, the Football (Offences) Act 1991, the Football (Offences and Disorder) Act 1999, the Football Spectators Act 1989, the Hunting Act 2004, the London Local Authorities Act 1990, the Safety of Sports Grounds Act 1975, and the Fire Safety and Safety of Places of Sport Act 1987.

*Related topic(s): ADMINISTRATIVE LAW; ANIMAL LAW; ARBITRATION and DISPUTE RESOLUTION; COMPETITION LAW; CONTRACT LAW; CRIMINAL LAW; INTELLECTUAL PROPERTY LAW; LOCAL GOVERNMENT LAW; TORT LAW; TRADE MARKS.*

| Author(s) | Title | Edition | Publisher | Year |
|---|---|---|---|---|
| Gardiner, Simon, *et al.* | *Sports Law* [S,P] | 5th | Routledge | 2016 |
| Randall, Nicholas | *Grayson's Sport and the Law* [P,N] | 4th | Bloomsbury Professional | 2016 |
| Gardiner, Simon | *Sports Law in the United Kingdom* [P,A] | | Kluwer Law International | 2014 |
| Lewis, Adam and Taylor, Jonathan, eds. | *Sport: Law and Practice* [P] | 3rd | Bloomsbury Professional | 2014 |
| James, Mark | *Sports Law* [S] | 2nd | Palgrave-Macmillan | 2013 |
| Anderson, Jack | *Modern Sports Law: A Textbook* [S] | | Hart Publishing | 2010 |
| Russ, Tim and Foster, Jamie | *Law of Field Sports* [N,P] | | Wildy, Simmonds & Hill | 2010 |

| Author(s) | Title | Edition | Publisher | Year |
|---|---|---|---|---|
| Hartley, Hazel | *Sport, Physical Recreation, and the Law* [A] | | Routledge | 2009 |
| Verow, Richard, Lawrence, Clive, and McCormick, Peter | *Sports Business: Law, Practice, and Precedents* [P] | 2nd | Jordan Publishing | 2005 |
| Kevan, Tim, Adamson, Dominic, and Cottrell, Stephen | *Sports Personal Injury: Law and Practice* [P] | | Sweet & Maxwell | 2002 |

## STATUTORY INTERPRETATION and LEGISLATIVE DRAFTING

As statutes are a fundamental source of English law the rules of interpreting legislation and works dealing with how they are best drafted are singularly important. Most such works deal with the place of courts in interpreting statutes, the different criteria and various rules to employ in interpreting legislation, the rules with regard to subordinate legislation, and the canons of legislative drafting.

The most salient statutes to note are the Interpretation Act 1978 and the Statutory Instruments Act 1946.

*Related topic(s): CONSTITUTIONAL LAW; CROWN LAW; DRAFTING and LEGAL WRITING; ENGLISH LEGAL SYSTEM; LEGAL SKILLS and METHOD; LOCAL GOVERNMENT LAW.*

| Author(s) | Title | Edition | Publisher | Year |
|---|---|---|---|---|
| Potter, Charlie and Lowe, David | *Understanding Legislation* [P,S] | | Hart Publishing | 2016 |
| Jones, Oliver and Bennion Francis A.R. | *Bennion on Statutory Interpretation* [P,A] | 6th | LexisNexis Butterworths | 2013 |
| Xanthaki, Helan | *Thornton's Legislative Drafting* [P,A] | 5th | Bloomsbury Professional | 2013 |
| Duxbury, Neil | *Elements of Legislation* [S,A] | | Cambridge University Press | 2012 |
| Ekins, Richard | *The Nature of Legislative Intent* [A] | | Oxford University Press | 2012 |
| Greenberg, Daniel | *Craies on Legislation: A Practitioner's Guide to the Nature, Process, Effect, and Interpretation of Legislation* [P,A] | 10th | Sweet & Maxwell | 2012* |
| Bennion, Francis A.R. | *Understanding Common Law Legislation: Drafting and Interpretation* [S,P,A] | | Oxford University Press | 2009 |
| McLeod, Ian | *Principles of Legislative and Regulatory Drafting* [S,P] | | Hart Publishing | 2009 |
| Bell, John and Engle, Sir George | *Statutory Interpretation* [P,A] | 3rd | LexisNexis Butterworths | 1995 |

## TAXATION

There are numerous types of taxation in the United Kingdom including (but not limited to) income tax, council tax, value added tax, corporate tax, capital gains tax, inheritance tax, and stamp duty (a tax on the purchase of real estate). The great majority of titles listed here deal with income tax, but some deal with other types of taxes and with the legal concepts of taxation in general.

Taxation is a legislation-based area of law and significant statutes include the Income Tax Act 2007, the Capital Gains Tax Act 1979, the Corporation Tax Act 2009, the Corporation Tax Act 2010, the Inheritance Tax Act 1984, the Stamp Act 1891, and the Value Added Tax Act 1994. There are also many related statutory instruments and a vast body of interpretive case law.

*Related topic(s): COMMERCIAL LAW; CRIMINAL LAW; EMPLOYMENT AND LABOUR LAW; LOCAL GOVERNMENT LAW; WILLS and PROBATE.*

| Author(s) | Title | Edition | Publisher | Year |
|---|---|---|---|---|
| Chamberlain, Emma, Whitehouse, Chris, and Greenfield, Roy, eds. | *Dymond's Capital Taxes* [P] | | Sweet & Maxwell | LL |
| Potter, D.C. and Monroe, H.H. | *Potter and Monroe's Tax Planning with Precedents* [P] | | Sweet & Maxwell | LL |
| Sherry, Michael, ed. | *Whiteman & Sherry on Capital Gains Tax* [P] | 5th | Sweet & Maxwell | LL |
| Stanley, Oliver | *Stanley: Taxation of Farmers and Landowners* [P] | | LexisNexis Butterworths | LL |
| Cordara, Roderick, ed. | *Tolley's Orange Tax Handbook 2016-17* [P] | | LexisNexis Butterworths | Annual |
| Dodwell, Bill and Prosser, Kevin, eds. | *The Green Book 2015-16* [P] | | CCH Editions | Annual |
| Dodwell, Bill and Prosser, Kevin, eds. | *The Red Book 2015-16* [8 volumes] [P] | | CCH Editions | Annual |
| Dolton, Alan and Walton, Kevin | *Tolley's Tax Cases 2015* [P] | | LexisNexis Butterworths | Annual |
| Dolton, Alan, Davis, Rhianon, and Rudling, David | *Tolley's VAT Cases 2015* [P] | | LexisNexis Butterworths | Annual |

| Author(s) | Title | Edition | Publisher | Year |
|---|---|---|---|---|
| Drysdale, Donald , *et al.* | *Core Tax Annuals: Income Tax 2015/16* [8 vols.] [P] | | Bloomsbury Professional | Annual |
| Drysdale, Donald | *Core Tax Annuals: Corporation Tax* [P] | | Bloomsbury Professional | Annual |
| Hayes, Claire and Newman, Ruth | *Tolley's Tax Guide 2016-17* [P] | | LexisNexis Butterworths | Annual |
| Lee, Natalie, ed. | *Revenue Law: Principles and Practice* [P,S] | | Bloomsbury Professional | Annual |
| McLaughlin, Mark, Harris, Toby, and Wunschmann-Lyall, Iris | *Core Tax Annuals: Inheritance Tax* [P] | | Bloomsbury Professional | Annual |
| Needham, Andrew | *Core Tax Annuals: Value Added Tax 205/16* [P] | | Bloomsbury Professional | Annual |
| Walton, Kevin | *Tolley's Capital Gains Tax 2015/16* [P] | | LexisNexis Butterworths | Annual |
| Wunschmann-Lyall, Iris and Erwood, Chris | *Core Tax Annuals: Trusts and Estates 2015/16* [P] | | Bloomsbury Professional | Annual |
| Hamilton, Penny | *Hamilton on Tax Appeals* [P] | 2nd | Bloomsbury Professional | 2016 |
| Morse, Geoffrey and Williams, David | *Davies: Principles of Tax Law* [P] | 8th | Sweet & Maxwell | 2016 |
| Murray, Rebecca | *Tax Avoidance* [P] | 3rd | Sweet & Maxwell | 2016 |
| Chamberlain, Emma and Whitehouse, Chris | *Trust Taxation and Estate Planning* [P] | 4th | Sweet & Maxwell | 2014 |
| Maas, Robert | *Taxation of Employments* [P] | 16th | Bloomsbury Professional | 2014 |
| Nock, Reg | *Stamp Duty Land Tax* [P] | 9th | Law Society Publishing | 2011 |

## Noteworthy websites, blogs, etc.:

### WEBSITES

- Gray's Inn Tax Chambers (http://taxbar.com/)
- LexisNexis, Lexis Web: Tax (http://lexisweb.co.uk/groups/tax/default.aspx)

### BLOGS

- Bloomsbury Professional, Tax Blog (http://www.bloomsburytaxonline.com/blog/)

- Fieldfisher (firm), Tax Deductions Law Blog (http://taxdeductionsblog.fieldfisher.com/)
- David Quentin, David Quentin's Tax & Law Blog (http://dqtax.tumblr.com/)

## TELECOMMUNICATIONS LAW

Since the enactment of the Railways Act 1844 (7 & 8 Vict., cap. 85), section 13 of which dealt with electric telegraphs, telecommunications has been a highly regulated activity in the United Kingdom. Until 1984 most telecommunication service (primarily telegraph and telephone) was provided exclusively by the Post Office. This monopoly was removed in 1984 just as numerous other telecommunications devices and media were coming into being (i.e., communication over computer networks and mobile telephony) and the entire market was opened to competition.

The law in this area is almost entirely statute-based and can found primarily in the Communications Act 2003 (which repealed and largely replaced the foundational Telecommunications Act 1984) and the Wireless Telegraphy Act 2006, which deals with mobile phones and wireless computer access.

The regulation of this industry is the remit of the Secretary of State for Culture, Media, and Sport through the Office of Communications (OFCOM) which was established by the Office of Communications Act 2003. The mandate of OFCOM, according to section 3(1) of the Act is to:

(a) To further the interests of citizens in relation to communications matters; and
(b) To further the interests of consumers in relevant markets, where appropriate by promoting competition.

There is obviously a large international component to this topic and as such there are a number of relevant international treaties and conventions along with European Community regulations and directives.

*Related topic(s): ADMINISTRATIVE LAW; CONSUMER LAW; DATA PROTECTION; EUROPEAN UNION LAW; INFORMATION TECHNOLOGY LAW; MEDIA and ENTERTAINMENT LAW.*

| Author(s) | Title | Edition | Publisher | Year |
|---|---|---|---|---|
| Long, Colin | *Global Telecommunications Law and Practice* [P] | | Sweet & Maxwell | LL |
| Lloyd, Ian and Mellor, David | *Telecommunications Law* [S] | 2nd | Oxford University Press | 2013 |
| Scherer, Joachim, ed. | *Telecommunications Laws in Europe* [N,P] | | Bloomsbury Professional | 2013 |
| Walden, Ian, ed. | *Telecommunications Law and Regulation* [P,S] 🖱 | 4th | Oxford University Press | 2012 |

| Author(s) | Title | Edition | Publisher | Year |
|---|---|---|---|---|
| Conradi, Mike, ed. | Communications Law Handbook [P] | | Bloomsbury Professional | 2009 |
| Koenig, Christian, *et al*, eds. | *EC Competition and Telecommunications Law* [P,A] | 2nd | Kluwer International | 2009 |

## Noteworthy websites, blogs, etc.:

### WEBSITE

- Office of Communications, Ofcom (http://www.ofcom.org.uk/)

### BLOG

- Rob Bratby, Watching the Connectives (http://robbratby.com/)

# TORT LAW

Tort law is the vast area of civil law under which parties who allege that they have sustained damage or loss by virtue of the actions or omissions of another. There are numerous examples of torts but the texts listed hereunder are those which provide treatment of the general concepts of tort law, such as what constitutes a tort, causation, severability, and remedies (primarily damages), although many do deal with individual torts.

A list of specific torts would include, but not be limited to: assault, battery, false imprisonment, libel and slander, malicious prosecution, misrepresentation, negligence, nuisance, trespass to goods, trespass to land, trespass to person, and wrongful interference with goods.

Tort is an ancient area of the common law and is based almost entirely in case law. There are very few statutes at play in tort although there is the Torts (Interference with Goods) Act 1997.

*Related topic(s): CONTRACT LAW; FRAUD and MISREPRESENTATION; HEALTH and SAFETY; LIBEL and SLANDER; LIMITATION; NEGLIGENCE; NUISANCE; PERSONAL INJURY LAW; PRIVACY LAW; REMEDIES, DAMAGES, and RESTITUTION.*

| Author(s) | Title | Edition | Publisher | Year |
|---|---|---|---|---|
| Goudkamp, James | *Tort Law Defences* [A,P] | | Hart Publishing | 2016 |
| Dyson, Andrew, Goudkamp, James, and Wilmot-Smith, Fred, eds. | *Defences in Tort* [A] | | Hart Publishing | 2015 |
| Horsey, Kirsty and Rackley, Dr Erika | *Tort Law* [S,A] | 4th | Oxford University Press | 2015 |
| Howarth, David, *et al.* | *Hepple and Matthews' Tort Law: Cases and Materials* [S,A] | 7th | Hart Publishing | 2015 |
| Kidner, Richard | *Casebook on Torts* [S] | 13th | Oxford University Press | 2015 |
| Rose, Francis, ed. | *Blackstone's Statutes on Contracts, Tort & Restitution 2015-16* [P,S] | | Oxford University Press | 2015* |
| Steel, Sandy | *Proof of Causation in Tort Law* [A] | | Cambridge University Press | 2015 |

| Author(s) | Title | Edition | Publisher | Year |
|---|---|---|---|---|
| Jones, Michael A., Dugdale, Anthony, and Simpson, Mark, eds. | *Clerk & Lindsell on Torts* [P,A] 🖱 | 21st | Sweet & Maxwell | 2014* |
| Peel, W. Edwin and Goudkamp, James | *Winfield & Jolowicz on Tort* [S,P,A] 🖱 | 19th | Sweet & Maxwell | 2014 |
| Steele, Jenny | *Tort Law: Text, Cases, and Materials* [S] 🖱 | | Oxford University Press | 2014 |
| Hedley, Stephen | *Tort* [S] | 7th | Oxford University Press | 2011 |
| Strong, S.I. and Williams, Liz | *Complete Tort Law: Text, Cases, and Materials* [S] | 2nd | Oxford University Press | 2011 |
| Lunney, Mark and Oliphant, Ken | *Tort Law: Text and Materials* [S] | 5th | Oxford University Press | 2013 |
| Deakin, Simon, Johnston, Angus, and Markesinis, Basil | *Markesinis and Deakin's Tort Law* [S] | 7th | Oxford University Press | 2012 |
| Harvey, Barbara and Marston, John | *Cases and Commentary on Tort* [S] | 6th | Oxford University Press | 2009 |
| Harpwood, Vivienne | *Modern Tort Law* [S] | 7th | Routledge-Cavendish | 2008 |

## Noteworthy websites, blogs, etc.:

### WEBSITE

- Stewart Dunn, The Law of Damages (http://www.stewartdunn.com/)

## TRADE MARKS

Considered a branch of intellectual property, a registered trade mark grants its owner traditional, proprietary property rights. A trade mark is that which provides the owner of a name and/or visual representation of a business or product the legal right to sole use of the mark. In order to be in effect and protected by law it must first be registered with the Comptroller General of Patents, Designs and Trade Marks (the Registrar).

This is an area of mixed common and statutory law with such legislative enactments as the Trade Marks Act 1994, the Hallmarking Act 1973, and the Companies Act 2006 (sections of which deal with business names) being instructive.

The primary issues in trade mark law are the registration process, the responsibilities of the registrar, the role of trade mark agents, altering or abandoning a trade mark, hallmarks and business names, infringement and passing-off, and the remedies available under each.

*Related topic(s): COMMERCIAL LAW; DESIGNS; INTELLECTUAL PROPERTY LAW; PROPERTY LAW.*

| Author(s) | Title | Edition | Publisher | Year |
|---|---|---|---|---|
| | *The Trade Mark Handbook* [P] | | Sweet & Maxwell | LL |
| Firth, Alison, Lea, Gary, and Cornford, Peter | *Trade Marks Law and Practice* [P] | 4th | Jordan Publishing | 2016 |
| Mellor, James, et al. | *Kerly's Law of Trade Marks and Trade Names* [P] | 16th | Sweet & Maxwell | 2016 |
| Morcom, Christopher, Roughton, Ashley, and St. Quintin, Thomas | *The Modern Law of Trade Marks* [P,A] | 5th | LexisNexis Butterworths | 2016 |
| Wilkof, Neil J. and Burkitt, Daniel | *Trade Mark Licensing* [P] | 3rd | Sweet & Maxwell | 2016 |
| Caddick, Nicholas and Longstaff, Ben | *A User's Guide to Trade Marks and Passing Off* [N] | 4th | Bloomsbury Professional | 2015 |
| Michaels, Amanda | *A Practical Guide to Trade Mark Law* [P,S] | 5th | Oxford University Press | 2014 |

| Author(s) | Title | Edition | Publisher | Year |
|---|---|---|---|---|
| Cornish, William R. and Llewelyn, David | Intellectual Property: Patents, Copyright, Trade Marks, and Allied Rights [S,P,A] | 8th | Sweet & Maxwell | 2013 |
| Wadlow, Christopher | *The Law of Passing-Off: Unfair Competition by Misrepresentation* [P,A] | 4th | Sweet & Maxwell | 2011* |

## Noteworthy websites, blogs, etc.:

### BLOGS

- Mark Anderson, IP Draughts (https://ipdraughts.wordpress.com/)
- Fieldfisher (firm), Intellectual Property Blog (http://intellectualpropertyblog.fieldfisher.com/)
- LexisNexis, World of IP and IT (WIPIT) Blog (http://blogs.lexisnexis.co.uk/wipit/)
- Shireen Smith, Azrights News and Media (www.venables.co.uk/blogs.htm)
- Neil J. Wilkof, et al., The IPKat (www.ipkat.com)

# WILLS and PROBATE

It is through wills (and codicils to wills) that a person makes provision for the distribution of one's assets after death. It is a well-developed area of primarily common law which imposes numerous formalities upon this process. While grounded solidly in a wealth of jurisprudence, there are some key statutes to note including the Administration of Estates Act 1925, the Administration of Estates Act 1971, the Trustee Act 1925, the Trustee Act 2000, the Family Law Reform Acts of 1969 and 1987, and the Inheritance (Provisions for Family and Dependants) Act 1975. A handful of sections of the Wills Act 1837 remain in force.

Texts which deal with wills and estates usually touch upon the following subtopics: the capacity of the testator, formalities of the will, the construction of the will, the powers and responsibilities of executors, probate and opposition to probate, the effects of intestacy, and the administration and distribution of the assets.

*Related topic(s): DRAFTING and LEGAL WRITING; EQUITY & TRUSTS; FAMILY LAW; FRAUD and MISREPRESENTATION; PROPERTY LAW.*

| Author(s) | Title | Edition | Publisher | Year |
|---|---|---|---|---|
| King, Lesley and Whitehouse, Christopher | *Tolley's Administration of Estates* [P] | | LexisNexis Butterworths | LL |
| Withers LLP, ed. | *Practical Wills Precedents* [P] | | Sweet & Maxwell | LL |
| Wright, Cherry E., ed. | *Butterworths Wills Probate and Administration Service* [P] | | LexisNexis Butterworths | LL |
| McKie, Simon and McKie, Sharon | *Tolley's Estate Planning 2015-16* [P] | | LexisNexis Butterworths | Annual |
| Francis, Andrew | *Contentious Probate Claims* [P] | 2nd | Sweet & Maxwell | 2016 |
| Kerridge, Roger and Brierly, A.H.R. | *Parry and Kerridge: The Law of Succession* [P] | 13th | Sweet & Maxwell | 2016 |
| Martyn, John Ross, *et al.* | *Theobald on Wills* [P] | 18th | Sweet & Maxwell | 2016 |
| Pearce, Nasreen | *A Practitioner's Guide to Probate Disputes* [P] | | Wildy, Simmonds & Hill | 2016 |
| Thurston, John | *A Practitioner's Guide to Executorship and Administration* [P] | 8th | Bloomsbury Professional | 2016 |

| Author(s) | Title | Edition | Publisher | Year |
|---|---|---|---|---|
| D'Costa, Roland, Teverson, Paul, and Synak, Terry | *Tristram and Coote's Probate Practice* [P] | 31st | LexisNexis Butterworths | 2015* |
| Barlow, Francis, *et al.*, eds. | *Williams on Wills* [P,A] | 9th | LexisNexis Butterworths | 2014 |
| Goodman, Dawn, Hewitt, Paul, and Mason, Henrietta | *Probate Disputes and Remedies* [P] | 3rd | Jordan Publishing | 2014 |
| King, Lesley and Gausden, Peter | *Wills: A Practical Guide* [P] | | Wildy, Simmonds & Hill | 2011 |
| King, Lesley | *Probate Practitioner's Handbook* [P] | 6th | The Law Society | 2010 |
| King, Lesley, Biggs, Keith, and Gausden, Peter | *A Practitioner's Guide to Wills* | 3rd | Wildy, Simmonds & Hill | 2010 |
| Chamberlain, Emma, Whitehouse, Chris | *Pre-Owned Assets and Estate Planning* [P] | 3rd | Sweet & Maxwell | 2009 |

## Noteworthy websites, blogs, etc.:

### WEBSITE

- LexisNexis, Lexis Web: Wills & Probate (http://lexisweb.co.uk/groups/wills-probate/default.aspx)

### BLOGS

- Clutton Cox (firm), Probate blog (http://www.cluttoncox.co.uk/site/blog/probateblog/)
- Clutton Cox (firm), Wills blog (http://www.cluttoncox.co.uk/site/blog/willsblog/)
- Society of Trust and Estate Practitioners, The STEP Blog (http://blog.step.org/about-2/)